Public Policy Writing
That Matters

Public Policy Writing
That Matters

Second Edition

David Chrisinger

Foreword by Katherine Baicker

JOHNS HOPKINS UNIVERSITY PRESS
Baltimore

Johns Hopkins University Press
2715 North Charles Street
Baltimore, Maryland 21218-4363
www.press.jhu.edu

Library of Congress Cataloging-in-Publication Data

Names: Chrisinger, David, 1986– author.
Title: Public policy writing that matters / David Chrisinger.
Description: Second edition. | Baltimore : Johns Hopkins University Press,
    2022. | Includes bibliographical references and index.
Identifiers: LCCN 2021006378 | ISBN 9781421442327 (paperback) |
    ISBN 9781421442334 (ebook)
Subjects: LCSH: Communication in public administration. | Communication
    in politics. | Written communication. | Persuasion (Rhetoric)—Political
    aspects.
Classification: LCC JF1525.C59 C35 2022 | DDC 808.06/632—dc23
LC record available at https://lccn.loc.gov/2021006378

A catalog record for this book is available from the British Library.

*Special discounts are available for bulk purchases of this book. For more information,
please contact Special Sales at specialsales@jh.edu.*

Modern English, especially written English, is full of bad habits which spread by imitation and which can be avoided if one is willing to take the necessary trouble. If one gets rid of these habits one can think more clearly, and to think clearly is a necessary first step towards political regeneration: so that the fight against bad English is not frivolous and is not the exclusive concern of professional writers.

—George Orwell, "Politics and the English Language"

Contents

Foreword

Dr. Katherine Baicker

We knew we were trying to answer an incredibly important policy question and that our results were going to get a lot of attention, but none of us knew quite what we were walking into. I was helping to lead a landmark study of the effects of health insurance coverage for low-income adults—a randomized controlled evaluation of Medicaid that had never been done, even though the program had been around since the mid-1960s. We published our results in leading academic journals—from the *New England Journal of Medicine* to *Science* to the *Quarterly Journal of Economics*. We were experts in constructing robust scientific findings and conveying them to experts, but connecting to a broader audience requires a different kind of expertise.

The results we found were nuanced. After comparing health care use, health, finances, and other outcomes for more than 6,300 adults who were randomly selected to apply for Medicaid coverage with another group of more than 5,800 who were not, we found that Medicaid coverage in the first two years generated no significant improvement in the physical health outcomes we measured. For example, we saw no detectable effect on blood pressure, cholesterol, obesity, or diabetic blood sugar control. At the same time, we found an increase in the use of health care across settings, a reduction in financial strain, lower rates of depression, and higher rates of diabetes detection and management.[1]

These much-anticipated findings generated a flurry of stories from leading newspapers, magazines, and think tanks of various political persuasions. Annie Lowrey in the *New York Times* led with "Medicaid Access Increases Use of Care, Study Finds,"[2] and Ezra Klein, writing for the *Washington Post,* noted that "Medicaid works as health insurance."[3] Writing for the Oregon Center for Public Policy, Chuck Sheketoff concluded that the lesson from our study was clear: "Medicaid works."[4] On the other side of the political spectrum, Michael F. Cannon of the Cato Institute wrote that "the nation's top health economists released a study that throws a huge 'stop' sign in front of ObamaCare's Medicaid expansion."[5] Michael Tanner, also of Cato, relied on the study to advocate against expanding Medicaid in Kansas.[6] Avik Roy wrote in an article published by *Forbes*, "The authors of the Oregon study published their updated, two-year results, finding that Medicaid 'generated no significant improvement in measured physical health outcomes.' The result calls into question the $450 billion a year we spend on Medicaid, and the fact that Obamacare throws 11 million more Americans into this broken program."[7] My favorite headline came from the *Atlantic*: "How to Use the Oregon Medicaid Study to Your Ideological Advantage."[8]

These divergent interpretations highlighted something important in communicating effectively to a wider audience. Almost every policy is going to have a wide range of effects, and those effects are going to be different for different people. It's easy to tell part of the story, cherry-picking anecdotes to match a particular view, even if only a small minority of people had that experience. In an article published in *Health Affairs* in 2016, my colleague Amy Finkelstein and I pointed out that you can find a compelling, true story to illustrate diametrically opposed cases.[9] We even made a quiz using actual quotes from study participants to show this. The anecdotes are really interesting, but they can point you in exactly the wrong direction.

This conundrum leads many academics to eschew storytelling altogether. But if we do that, we give up on so much of the impact that our research might have. Rock-solid evidence is important, of course, and so is our ability to stay true to the evidence and bring it to life through storytelling. Never straying from the conclusions that the data support requires real discipline. And turning those conclusions into a narrative that can influence people who aren't experts requires real dedication. Not every researcher will invest the time and energy to create those broadly accessible, persuasive narratives, but if you care about making a difference, that's time well spent.

This is a lesson I've brought with me to the University of Chicago's Harris School of Public Policy, where we believe that the solutions to today's most complex problems must be grounded in evidence but that real impact can only come with compelling communication of that evidence. Our Medicaid study provided evidence to refute both the unduly optimistic and unduly pessimistic views of the program that had dominated the debate around the 2010 Affordable Care Act. And both views had anecdotes to support them. We had the facts, but we had to tell people about them effectively enough to cut through the noise and influence a roiling public debate.

The decision makers who will someday read your work won't necessarily be well versed in statistics and economics. To be an effective policy analyst, you must be comfortable running regression analyses as well as communicating your findings to someone who does not understand what a regression analysis is. The core curriculum in a place like the Harris School will help you master the former, and this book will help you master the latter.

Dr. Katherine Baicker serves as the dean and Emmet Dedmon Professor at the University of Chicago's Harris School of Public Policy. She is an elected member of the National Academy of Medicine, the National Academy of Social Insurance, the Council on Foreign Relations, and the American Academy of Arts and Sciences. Dr. Baicker also holds appointments as a research associate at the National Bureau of Economic Research and as an affiliate of the Abdul Latif Poverty Action Lab. She also serves on the Congressional Budget Office's Panel of Health Advisers and on the board of directors of Eli Lilly, HMS, NORC, and the Mayo Clinic. Before coming to the University of Chicago, Dr. Baicker was the C. Boyden Gray Professor of Health Economics in the Department of Health Policy and Management at the Harvard T. H. Chan School of Public Health. From 2005 to 2007, she served as a Senate-confirmed member of the president's Council of Economic Advisers, where she played a leading role in the development of health policy. Dr. Baicker earned her BA in economics from Yale and her PhD in economics from Harvard.

Public Policy Writing
That Matters

Introduction

I know nothing about the identity of the whistleblower who submitted an official complaint to Senator Richard Burr and Representative Adam Schiff regarding President Donald J. Trump's phone call on July 25, 2019, with Ukrainian president Volodymyr Zelensky. What I do know is that, in just nine short pages, the whistleblower laid out a concise and revelatory narrative of bracing clarity that alleged the Trump administration had tried to cover up a damaging record of the president trying to coerce a foreign government into meddling in the 2020 election by investigating the son of Joseph R. Biden Jr., a Democrat who would later be elected the next president of the United States. The result of the whistleblower's complaint was the 2019 impeachment of President Trump.

If you're even half as passionate as I am about what makes a policy story matter, perhaps you're wondering what made the complaint such an interesting and persuasive read. How is it possible, you might ask, that a mere nine-page complaint could lead Speaker Nancy Pelosi to announce that the US House of Representatives would start a formal impeachment inquiry when, months before, the equally troubling findings of a two-year investigation led by Special Counsel Robert Mueller did not? Put another way: How can we, as policy analysts and writers, ensure that we are ready to tell a story that *really* matters when the time comes?

There are several important lessons on policy storytelling we can glean from the whistleblower. First, and perhaps most important, the whistleblower's complaint begins with the main, unequivocal point: "The President of the United States is using the power of his office to solicit interference from a foreign country in the 2020 U.S. election."[1]

By starting with the main point, the whistleblower wisely avoids boring the reader with pleasantries or difficult-to-slog-through background.

Second, the whistleblower clarifies *why* they felt it necessary to tell this story now: "I am deeply concerned that the actions described below constitute a 'serious or flagrant problem, abuse, or violation of law or Executive Order' that 'does not include differences of opinion concerning public policy matters,' consistent with the definition of an 'urgent concern.'" The president had allegedly abused his power. And this, by definition, is an urgent concern because such an action poses risks to national security and undermines efforts to deter and counter foreign interference in US elections. The whistleblower then writes that they are fulfilling their duty to report what they know, "through proper legal channels, to the relevant authorities."[2] If we stopped reading right there, we would know nearly everything needed to understand what was happening, why it was important, and why the story was being told now.

Contrast this clarity and concision with the heavily redacted 448-page *Report on the Investigation into Russian Interference in the 2016 Presidential Election* issued by the special counsel. The special counsel's report begins with the main point, "The Russian government interfered in the 2016 presidential election in sweeping and systematic fashion," before laying out facts for and against whether the president obstructed justice by attempting to derail the investigation. Ultimately, the special counsel did not reach a conclusion on that matter. Instead, he arrived at a confusing and inconclusive judgment: "while this report does not conclude that the President committed a crime, it also does not exonerate him."[3] For many, the story of what happened during and a few months after the 2016 election was no clearer than it was before the special counsel began his investigation. Lacking clear findings, Mueller's work had virtually no impact.

Besides its equivocal findings, the sheer amount of evidence and analysis included in the report was unmanageable. Unsurprisingly, only a small segment of American lawmakers read the full report. At the end of May 2019, about two months after publication of the special counsel's report, Representative Jerrold Nadler, a Democrat from New York, said he believed there was justification for launching impeachment proceedings against the president, but he cautioned that the public must first agree that it's warranted. "The American people," he said at the time, did not support impeachment "because they do not know the story. They don't know the facts."[4]

Much of what the country learned by way of "facts" came from Attorney General William Barr's four-page summary of the report. The evidence developed during the special counsel's investigation, Barr concluded, was "not sufficient to establish that the President committed an obstruction-of-justice offense."[5] Even though Mueller's office had built a persuasive case for Trump's having committed obstruction of justice, Mueller said nothing of the sort in his report. According to Jeffrey Toobin, who reconstructed the Mueller investigation for the *New Yorker* to explain why it was so ineffectual, "Mueller forfeited the opportunity to speak clearly and directly about Trump's crimes, and Barr filled the silence with his high-volume exoneration." Though not technically inaccurate, Toobin continues, Barr's letter "spun the special counsel's findings about Russia in a way that was favorable to Trump."[6] On March 27, 2019, Mueller wrote to Barr and pointed out that Barr's letter "did not fully capture the context, nature, and substance" of his office's conclusions.[7]

Nearly 17 months later, a Republican-controlled Senate panel published a nearly thousand-page report that confirmed some of Robert Mueller's findings. First, the Russian government sabotaged the 2016 presidential election to help Donald Trump become president. Second, several advisors in Trump's campaign were receptive to such help. "This is what collusion looks like," Senate Democrats wrote.[8] Besides confirming much of what the special council's 2019 report detailed, the Senate Intelligence Committee's report, according to the *Washington Post*, contains "dozens of new findings that appear to show more direct links between Trump associates and Russian intelligence, and it pierces the president's long-standing attempts to dismiss the Kremlin's intervention on his behalf as a hoax."[9]

Let's turn back to the whistleblower's complaint for a moment. Besides starting with the main point and being crystal clear about the *why* behind the complaint, the whistleblower also uses clear headings to help the reader navigate the contents of the complaint. In the first section, under the heading "The 25 July Presidential phone call," the whistleblower orients the reader by laying out when the call took place and with whom the president spoke. The whistleblower is clear about what is known:

1. *What the whistleblower knows*: "After an initial exchange of pleasantries, the President used the remainder of the call to advance his personal interests."
2. *How the whistleblower knows it*: "Multiple White House officials with direct knowledge of the call informed me."
3. *What the whistleblower does not know*: "I do not know which side initiated the call."[10]

After laying out the details of the president's call and what was alarming about it, the whistleblower moves on to "efforts to restrict access to records related to the call" and then to "ongoing concerns," including the fact that the US special representative for Ukraine negotiations, Kurt Volker, visited the Ukrainian capital the day after the president's call to meet with a variety of Ukrainian political figures and help them " 'navigate' the demands that the President had made."[11]

In the fourth and final section of the complaint, the whistleblower walks the reader, step by step, through the time line that led to the president's call on July 25. The central character of this section is Rudolph "Rudy" Giuliani, the president's personal lawyer, whom the US State Department saw as a "rogue" operator and a potential threat to national security. The whistleblower recounts the struggles that senior American diplomats had in dealing with the confusion created by Giuliani's efforts to pressure Ukrainian officials into developing compromising information about Joe Biden and his son.

In the weeks that followed the release of the whistleblower's complaint, virtually every piece of evidence presented in the complaint was corroborated by the White House's reconstructed transcript of the call with President Zelensky or by the congressional testimony and documents provided by current and former administration officials. The president solicited interference. He froze aid to Ukraine. Both Giuliani and Attorney General Barr were involved. They put national security at risk. And White House officials knew the call was, at the very least, problematic, which is why they placed the transcript of the call in a highly classified computer system normally reserved for documents related to covert operations.

At a granular level, the whistleblower's complaint provides excellent examples of strong sentences with clear subjects (who or what the sentence is about, *italicized* below) and active verbs (what action is taking place in the sentence, **bolded** below):

- *"The President* **pressured** Mr. Zelensky."
- *"The President* also **praised** Ukraine's Prosecutor General, Mr. Yuriy Lutsenko, and **suggested** that Mr. Zelensky might want to keep him in this position."
- *"Senior White House officials* **had intervened** to 'lock down' all records of the phone call."
- *"Mr. Giuliani* reportedly **traveled** to Madrid to meet with one of President Zelensky's advisers."

If you were to close your eyes after reading the sentences above, I doubt you'd have any trouble picturing exactly *who* was doing *what*. In this case, clear writing by the whistleblower leads to clear thinking for the reader.

If the question of what makes public policy writing *really* matter can be answered so easily, why is so much of what policy analysts write still weighed down with muddled analysis, overly detailed explanations, methodological jargon, complex sentence structures, and incoherent paragraphs?

The primary reason is that many policy analysts misunderstand the purpose of policy writing. I don't blame them—and they shouldn't blame themselves, either. If your undergraduate or graduate education was anything like mine, you were probably taught how to analyze data and evidence, develop an original argument, and situate that argument within a broader field of research. The focus of your writing was probably on theory, not necessarily on application. That's mostly what academics do. They *think* about how to think about things. And during the time we were students of these academics, our job was to produce a nuanced account of concepts and principles to show them we had mastered the content and debates in our chosen discipline.

The problem is that those who aren't familiar with our disciplines often struggle to understand what it is we're trying to say. This isn't a new problem or one that exists only in the academy, either. Soon after the Second World War ended, the famed novelist and essayist George

Orwell argued that "modern English, especially written English, is full of bad habits which spread by imitation" and that much of what passed for political writing in Great Britain was "ugly."[12] Twenty years after Orwell published his critique, John O'Hayre wrote *Gobbledygook Has Gotta Go* to teach his fellow Bureau of Land Management employees how to avoid "outdated, outmoded, tradition-logged language based on an outdated, outmoded, tradition-logged philosophy of communication," which had resulted in the convoluted writing that made government documents impossible to comprehend.[13] A few years later, President Richard M. Nixon began requiring the *Federal Register*—a daily publication that issues the proposed and final administrative regulations of federal agencies—to be written in "layman's terms."[14] Echoing Orwell's argument that writing needed to be simplified to free the writer "from the worst follies of orthodoxy," President William "Bill" Clinton issued an executive order in 1998 that required all federal employees to use short sentences, the active voice, and "common, everyday words."[15]

More recently, President Barack Obama signed into law the Plain Writing Act of 2010. Aimed at improving "the effectiveness and accountability of Federal agencies," the Plain Writing Act promotes "clear Government communication that the public can understand and use."[16] The purpose of the act, according to those who wrote it, was to incentivize federal agencies to give the American people information they can understand in an effort to increase trust between the government and its citizenry. How can you trust a person or an institution if you do not understand what they are saying?

The purpose of policy writing, therefore, is much more reader-focused than academic writing. As policy analysts, we no longer have to concern ourselves with developing an original thesis statement and arguing about theory with an audience of experts poised to dispute our thesis. Instead, our purpose is to understand what our readers *need* to know to fulfill their mission or achieve their goals and then to provide them with interesting policy stories, based on persuasive evidence and rigorous data analysis and told with integrity to the facts. If you can do all that, you can then rest assured that you did all you could do. The remainder is up to the audience and, unfortunately, the powers that be.

I wish I could give you a magic formula to follow that would inspire all the changes you want to see in the world. But I can't. And anyone who says they can is only telling you what you want to hear. The whistleblower fulfilled their responsibilities. They told a clear and concise story based on robust evidence. That should have been enough to lead to the conviction of the president. But it wasn't. You won't interrupt the historical record, or persuade a reader skeptical of your claims, every time your fingers hit the keyboard. But that doesn't mean you and I shouldn't try. To paraphrase President Obama, who faced impenetrable obstruction by a Republican-controlled Congress for much of his time in office, I'd rather get caught trying than wallowing in the self-pity of defeat.

I'm going to show you how to try. In part I, we'll discuss the purpose of policy analysis and communication and the unique needs of our readers. I'll tell you what to do if you ever find yourself writing around holes in your story. You cannot expect to write clearly if you haven't first thought clearly about your work. So I'm going to show you one way to organize your thinking before you start writing.

In part II, I'll introduce you to several human-centered design tools that I have found incredibly useful for organizing thoughts and evidence into a coherent structure. These tools are especially helpful in making sure that the people—and the politics—that will be impacted by a change in policy remain in the front of your mind throughout your researching and writing. I'll also show you how to use a dramatic arc to tell vivid and compelling policy stories that will haunt your reader by drawing them in and sticking with them afterward.

If you're experienced in policy analysis and are looking specifically for instruction on the craft of policy storytelling, you may want to start with part III. In addition to showing you how to structure a policy memo or brief for maximum impact, I'll teach you how to construct coherent paragraphs with strong topic sentences and to compose clear and concise sentences that help your reader understand who is doing what.

In part IV, I'll explain how to be your own best editor, and in part V, we'll cover the finishing touches. I'll show you how to quote from and paraphrase your sources properly, and my colleague James Bennett will show you how to develop data visualizations that can make your policy story more persuasive. And for those who have ever wondered how to format bulleted lists or ensure that all little style and grammar issues are taken care of before you hit "send" on that final draft, you'll appreciate the final chapter.

Since I finished writing the first edition of this book, two big things in my life have changed. First, I left my job at the Government Accountability Office to build a policy writing program at the University of Chicago's Harris School of Public Policy. When I was still working for the federal government, I was not allowed to write about any of the topics I had worked on, nor was I allowed to write anything that could call my political independence into question. Truth be told, I found such restrictions silly. Regardless, I am no longer bound by them.

Second, I started teaching graduate students—not early- and mid-career policy analysts—how to write about public policy. The greatest difference I found between the two groups was that most of my students not only needed help learning how to write more effectively, but they also needed instruction on how to *think* about their writing. After hundreds of one-on-one coaching sessions with my students, I realized that 90 percent of the time they were not struggling with paragraphs and sentences as much as they were struggling with clarifying what they were thinking and with conveying it well to their audience. In this second edition, I've included much more instruction on how to think about your writing before you invest hours and hours in writing a first draft. Clear writing, I found, cannot exist without clear thinking.

Admittedly, much of the writing advice included in this book is not new. Some of it may be new to you, of course, in which case I hope you find it helpful. If you are well versed in the study of professional writing, you will probably recognize the influence that several fantastic writing manuals have had on my development as a writer, editor, and teacher: William Strunk Jr. and E. B. White's *The Elements of Style*, William Zinsser's *On Writing Well*, Joseph M. Williams's *Style,* and Aaron Wildavsky's *Speaking Truth to Power*. I have translated and synthesized their sage advice into practical tips and tools specific to the stylistic requirements and limitations of policy writing. It's my hope that you'll read this book, dog-ear the pages most helpful to you, and pull it off the shelf each time you sit down to write public policy that matters.

Let's begin.

PART 1

The Thinking Behind
Effective Policy Analysis

CHAPTER 1

Clear Thinking Leads to Clear Writing

When I coach students one-on-one at the Harris School, many of them seek me out because they don't think they're talented writers. For some, English isn't their first language. For others, quantitative analysis comes easier than writing, which they'd avoided doing as much as was possible while in college. Nine times out of 10, though, they're dead wrong about their abilities as writers. What they struggle with is not the writing; it's the thinking *behind* their writing. When students come to me for help with a policy memo, for example, I'll start the coaching session by asking them what they want to recommend. They'll tell me something like "I want to recommend that the country pass a mandatory voting law with the goal of increasing voter turnout."

The next question I'll ask is about the causes of low voter turnout: Why don't people turn out to vote? Is it because they don't have to? That's when I start to see the wheels turning behind their eyes. There are, after all, many reasons why people may decide not to vote. If they're a journalist, for example, they may choose not to vote to appear more neutral or independent. Or maybe someone doesn't vote because they cannot get time off from work. Or maybe they live too far from their polling place and have no access to reliable transportation. We could probably spend the entire coaching session brainstorming reasons why someone wouldn't vote; it's like other types of policy challenges—incredibly complex and nuanced.

After we've established that there may be many reasons why something is happening, I'll ask them about the evidence they've collected. What does it tell us is happening? Is what is happening something desirable or undesirable? How do you know, I ask, what is desirable? This line of questioning is what good policy analysts do. They think before they write. They think about what questions need to be answered so that the reader can take those answers and solve a problem or address an issue.

In early summer 2020, soon after George Floyd was tragically tortured to death by a police officer named Derek Chauvin in Minneapolis, Minnesota, there was one policy question that had everyone talking: Should police departments be defunded? Those who advocate defunding argue that procedural tweaks—such as mandating that police officers complete implicit-bias training, hosting police-community listening sessions, creating civilian review boards, and updating use-of-force policies—won't be enough to fix policing in America, as evidenced by the fact that the officer who killed George Floyd had received 17 misconduct complaints over nearly two decades on the job, and not one of the procedural tweaks instituted by the Minneapolis Police Department had inspired him to improve his behavior or resulted in his removal from the force.

How can a policy analyst like you or me help inform this debate? First, we would need to define our terms. Then, we'd need to conduct rigorous data analysis that can inform our recommendations for reform. For some, defunding the police means making it easier to identify and prosecute police misconduct like Chauvin's. One way to do this, according to Peter Suderman, is to reform police unions, which, Suderman argues, "exist to demand that taxpayers pay for dangerous, and even deadly, negligence. And although they are not the only pathology that affects American policing, they are a key internal influence on police culture, a locus of resistance to improvements designed to reduce police violence."[1] Labor contracts negotiated by police unions around the country, for instance, generally impede accountability measures, according to the Police Union Contract Project, which collects and compares police union contracts. These contracts often prevent officers from being questioned soon after they are involved in an incident, require cities to pay legal fees and any financial settlements related to officers' misconduct, and limit disciplinary measures that can be taken against officers who abuse their power.[2]

In June 2020, prison abolitionist Mariame Kaba wrote an op-ed in which she argued unequivocally that the police cannot be reformed.

"The only way to diminish police violence," she claims, "is to reduce contact between the public and the police." Police officers, according to Kaba, "don't do what you think they do." Instead of chasing down violent criminals and making felony arrests, most of their time is spent "responding to noise complaints, issuing parking and traffic citations, and dealing with other noncriminal issues." If the number of police officers currently serving was cut in half, along with a similar-sized cut to their departmental budgets, she continues, police officers would have less power, which would result in fewer opportunities for them to "brutalize and kill people." It would also result in health care, housing, education, and employment training programs finally receiving the funding they need to be effective, which, Kaba argues, would ultimately lead to an entirely different social and economic order characterized, in part, by less crime and much less need for police. "We can build other ways of responding to harms in our society," she says. "Trained 'community care workers' could do mental health checks if someone needs help. Towns could use restorative-justice models instead of throwing people in prison."[3]

On the same day that the *New York Times* published Kaba's op-ed, a columnist for the *Washington Post*, Leana S. Wen, wrote about the need to reimagine public safety through what she called public health partnerships: "Instead of using the inflammatory language of 'defunding the police,' what if we consider a new approach to policing through partnering with public health efforts?" Thinking along these more constructive lines, where the vital role of the police is recognized and public health plays a larger role, Wen says, could lead not only to a reduction in crime but also in violence perpetrated by police officers.[4]

Only after we understand the terms of the debate can we formulate policy questions that can be answered. Figuring out what the right questions are—and providing persuasive answers—is *the* purpose of public policy writing that matters.

THE PURPOSE OF POLICY ANALYSIS

At the University of Chicago's Harris School of Public Policy, there is a large maroon banner with cream-colored bubble letters that greets all new students when they walk through the front doors of the building. It reads, "Your impact story starts here." At Harris, we talk a lot about impact. We want students to impact the world. We tell them we will teach them the quantitative skills they'll need to have impact. We promise them that once they graduate from the program, they'll be ready to change the world. Let that sink in for a moment. We're here to change the world. The expectations couldn't be higher.

Every time I see that sign, I get an anxious lump in my throat. And when I'm asked to teach first-year students how to write a policy memo that's "going to change the world," that anxious lump morphs into something much closer to panic. How can I even attempt such a thing in 90-minute workshops that students aren't even required to attend? The only thing that reduces this panic, I've found, is to set aside the goal of changing the world with policy writing and to reduce the purpose of policy communication to its simplest terms. If I were in charge of designing another banner for the Harris School, I'd consider a much bigger one that read,

> Your impact story starts with learning how to ask the right questions AND answer them with the most convincing evidence that rigorous data analysis can provide. Try not to worry so much about making an impact and changing the world . . . yet. That will come in due time. And when it comes, you'll be ready.

Too wordy, I know. I'm sure I could capture my internal monologue more concisely, though I'm not convinced a more concise version would have more of a punch. The point is that to be valuable policy analysts, we need to divorce ourselves from the idea that we're here to change the world. That's not to say our work *won't* change the world. Rather, we need to focus on what we can control and worry less about what we can't. What we can control are the questions we ask and the answers we provide. Think of it this way: Your readers have unanswered questions. Generally, they don't really know what's happening. They don't know why it's happening. And they don't know what to do to make a positive change.

That's where we come in. If we're able to figure out what questions we can answer for the readers and answer them with convincing evidence based on rigorous data analysis, we can help our readers solve a problem. Our readers taking the answers we give them to solve a problem is what will lead to impact. And if we're fortunate, that impact will change the world for the better.

THE THREE TYPES OF POLICY QUESTIONS

There are three types of policy questions that analysts need to answer to help their readers solve pressing problems:

1. What's happening?
2. What's working?
3. What should be done next?

That's it. In all my years working as a policy analyst and communicator, I have yet to encounter a policy question that wasn't some variation of one of these questions. I've also found that the most persuasive policy stories will answer all three.

Let's return to the question of whether police departments should be defunded by focusing on the city of Chicago. What are the questions readers might need answered before they can solve the policy problems posed by policing?

1. What's happening?

Before we get into more evaluative and prescriptive kinds of stories, we first need to understand, and clearly communicate to our readers, what is happening, who the key stakeholders are, and how we got to where we are today. Two questions about the Chicago Police Department immediately come to my mind:

1. How much funding does the Chicago Police Department receive each year?
2. How does the police department's annual budget compare with those for public health and social services provided by the city?

In answer to these questions, you'd find that for fiscal year 2020 (which began on January 1 in Chicago), the city allocated $1.7 billion to police the 2.7 million people who call Chicago home (17.2 percent of the city's $9.9 billion budget). That $1.7 billion is nearly double the amount of money the city spent on the fire department, public transportation, public libraries, and public health services combined.[5] One way you might interpret these numbers is to say that Chicago has decided to invest a significant sum of money in policing and has, in turn, deprioritized the public health and social services it could provide to help address potential root causes of crime and the need for police.

To put these figures into context, let's compare Chicago's budget to decisions made in New York City, the largest city in the United States with the largest police department in the country. For fiscal year 2020 (which began on July 1), New York City allocated $5.9 billion to its police department (6.7 percent of the city's $88.2 billion budget). At the same time, the city planned to spend

- $2.1 billion on services for people experiencing homelessness,
- $1.9 billion on public health,
- $1.3 billion on housing,
- $988 million on youth and community development, and
- $382 million on jobs programs.[6]

Next, we may want to ask questions about what happens when police officers respond to "calls for service," which include 911 calls, alarms, police radio dispatch, and nonemergency calls:

- What do police officers in Chicago encounter when they respond to calls for service?
- How are police officers generally deployed throughout the city?
- How are their districts staffed?

The data required to answer all three questions for Chicago do not exist or are not available to the public. We do know, however, that in three other American cities that post data online showing how their police officers spend their time, only about 4 percent of officers' time is spent handling violent crime, according to crime analysts Jeff Asher and Ben Horwitz. Police officers in New Orleans, Montgomery County (Maryland), and Sacramento spend about half their time responding to "noncriminal calls" and controlling traffic, and that's not even factoring in how much time is spent investigating, training, and completing administrative duties. "As experts continue to debate how best to improve the performance of law enforcement," Asher and Horowitz conclude, "it's helpful to first have a clear understanding of how the police spend their time interacting with the public, including how little of it revolves around responding to violent crime."[7] That's not to say, however, that police work is not inherently dangerous, regardless of whether officers are called to a violent crime. On some occasions police officers are called to a situation seemingly nonviolent that quickly devolves into violence through no fault of the officers.

We also know that, in the United States, the police arrest over 10 million people every year. Of those 10 million arrests, 80 percent are for relatively minor offenses such as drug possession or drinking in public. According to Christian Davenport, a professor at the University of Michigan, "People believe that the police are deterring violence . . . And that's highly questionable." In June 2020, he told Vox that there is plenty of research that suggests police officers are "having no influence whatsoever" on deterring violence. In addition, police officers are generally the first responders to emergencies related to mental health, and one in every four deaths from police shootings is of someone diagnosed with mental health problems. "I can literally imagine," he continues, replacing an armed officer "with someone who will actually sit down on the ground with them and talk. Not throw them on the ground and sit on top of them or lay on top of them. But someone who will take them wherever they are, listen to their situation and then try to figure out, diagnose their problem."[8] Some in the law enforcement community agree, such as former Dallas police chief David Brown: "Every societal failure, we put it off on the cops to solve. Not enough mental health funding, let the cops handle it. Not enough drug addiction funding, let's give it to the cops. Schools fail, give it to the cops. Policing was never meant to solve all those problems."[9]

As far as staffing goes, in 2016 the City of Chicago laid out a plan to hire an extra 516 officers, 92 field-training officers, 200 detectives, 112 sergeants, and 50 lieutenants over a two-year period.[10] When asked by the *Chicago Sun-Times* why the city needed so many new officers, Eddie Johnson, then police superintendent, said the mayor based the decision on a staffing analysis conducted by the department. "We did an overall analysis of the department . . . and this is what I think we need to make Chicago safer," he said.[11] By the end of summer 2020, however, the Chicago Police Department had not yet released a copy of this analysis, which makes it impossible for independent analysts to test the veracity of the department's findings. In early July 2020, after conducting a "good faith and reasonable search" of the department's files, the city said it could not find the staffing analysis. Shortly before this admission, according to a June 2020 independent monitoring report filed in court, the Chicago Police Department hired the University of Chicago Crime Lab, the Civic Consulting Alliance, and other experts to perform a new staffing analysis.[12] Before we can know how to move forward, policy analysts need these data and analysis.

2. What's working?

Once we have a sense of what the problem looks like on the ground, we can look to various interventions that have been tried and glean important lessons learned. One benefit of the United States having such a decentralized system of law enforcement is that we have thousands of "laboratories" (between 12,000 and 18,000 law enforcement departments across the country, depending on how you count them) where reforms can be piloted, evaluated, and iterated. While we don't have many—if any—definitive studies that specify what's working and what isn't, there are plenty of good studies we can draw inferences from and use to advocate for defunding police departments or for more traditional reforms. We might want to ask, for example,

- How effective is the current public safety model in Chicago?
- What other public safety models have been implemented around the country, and how effective have those models been?

Again, we would need to define what we mean by *public safety model*, and we'd also need to be clear about how we were going to evaluate effectiveness. Are we going to look at public satisfaction surveys? The number of calls for service that result in arrests? The number of officer-involved shootings? We could probably come up with dozens of indicators to measure that would help us show whether the police are operating effectively. I cannot tell you which indicators are best. That's something you as the analyst need to decide and communicate clearly.

As for other models of public safety that depart from Chicago's, there are plenty we could analyze. In 2007, for example, the health department in Baltimore, Maryland, developed a program called Safe Streets. The city hired people—many of whom had served time in prison—to mediate conflicts in their communities. In 2014, these mediators (also known as "violence interrupters") helped quell more than 880 conflicts, the vast majority of which were deemed likely to have resulted in gun violence. In one neighborhood where the mediators were active, homicides dropped by 56 percent. In another, they dropped by 26 percent.

As part of a national effort called Cure Violence, more than 50 communities in over 25 cities, including Chicago, have implemented a similar approach to violence prevention that does not depend on law enforcement.[13] In 2014, researchers found that in two neighborhoods in Chicago these interventions had resulted in a 31 percent greater decrease in killings and a 19 percent greater decrease in shootings.[14] "Violence does not happen randomly or in isolation," Leana S. Wen and M. Cooper Lloyd wrote in 2016 of Baltimore's public health initiatives. "It is one tragic, final result of inequities that continually build if left unaddressed. By treating it as a public health issue, it can be prevented—and, perhaps one day, even cured."[15]

In 2017, the City of Denver tried something new in the way it ensures public safety, and early evaluation results show this novel approach may work. The city created Crisis Intervention Response Units that pair police officers with mental health professionals. When someone in mental health distress in Denver calls 911, one of these units responds and treats the people they encounter more like patients than criminals. In 2018, the units encountered 1,725 people across the city. Police officers arrested only 3 percent of them; 2 percent were issued tickets. What was far more likely to happen was that these units connected the people with the Mental Health Center of Denver, where they received mental health support.[16] The units also connected people to housing resources and substance abuse disorder treatment.[17] "All of the folks involved in this program view this to be instrumental" to diverting people in a behavioral health crisis from going to jail, the

Crisis Intervention Response Units' spokesperson, Jeff Holliday, told the city's safety committee in December 2019.[18]

In August 2020, the RAND Corporation published a report on various policy options for reforming the way public safety is maintained in the United States. The common thread that ties them together is that they ask police to solve fewer of society's problems—especially those that law enforcement officers may not be well suited for. "The United States," the authors of the report claim, "has many societal problems that have very different (often complex and overlapping) causes and for which effective solutions require responses from practitioners with very specialized training, expertise, and resilience." Proponents of defunding the police, they continue, argue for allocating funding to service providers that can address both the "symptoms *and* the root causes" of homelessness, mental health crises, and substance abuse disorders, among other societal issues (table 1.1).[19]

The key here seems to be this: what those who call for defunding the police are really advocating is a reimagining of public safety and a re-prioritization of funding to pay for services that can help the people who are most likely to be harmed during interactions with law enforcement. This is key because if the police are defunded without such reimagining and re-prioritization of funding, the results could be disastrous. A case in point: In 2008, officials in Vallejo, California, defunded their police department by half after filing for bankruptcy during the Great Recession. "Far from ushering in a new era of harmony between police and the people," Peter Jamison wrote in the *Washington Post*, "the budget cuts worsened tensions between the department and the community and were followed by a dramatic surge in officers' use of deadly force. Since 2009 the police have killed 20 people, an extraordinarily high number for such a small city. In 2012 alone, officers fatally shot six suspects. Nearly a third of the city's homicides that year were committed by law enforcement." One thing Jamison initially failed to mention was that when Vallejo officials cut police funding in half, they did not provide additional funding for public health and social services agencies. "Defunding the police," then, must be a policy of presence, not just of absence.

It's also important to note that reallocating funds to public health and social services agencies may not necessarily lead to a less deadly

TABLE 1.1. The RAND Corporation's examples of policing functions that could be reallocated

Policing issue	Strategy with lesser enforcement role	Examples
Homelessness	• Homeless outreach teams • Law enforcement–assisted diversion (LEAD) • Housing interventions	• Chula Vista Homeless Outreach Teams; Seattle Navigation Teams; Community Outreach Resource Program, Indio, California • Seattle LEAD Program • Permanent supportive housing programs
Behavioral health	• Community-based behavioral health crisis response • Police-assisted substance use treatment • Police–mental health collaboratives	• Crisis Assistance Helping Out on the Streets • Police-Assisted Addiction and Recovery Initiative and angel initiatives • Crisis intervention teams' co-responder programs
Community violence	• Violence prevention initiatives • Community development • Advance counseling and mentoring for at-risk youth	• Cure Violence • Local nonprofit organizations • Becoming a Man
School safety	• Early intervention and prevention	• Positive behavioral interventions and supports • Threat assessment and prevention
Dispute resolution	• Coordinated community response models	• Domestic Violence Enhanced Response Team, Colorado Springs, Colorado
Traffic enforcement	• Shift responsibility to civilian departments of transportation	• Transportation Alternatives, New York; Berkeley, California, Department of Transportation

police force. Jamison quotes Danté R. Quick, the pastor at Vallejo's Friendship Missionary Baptist Church, who said, "Our police department is woefully 'defunded,' which has led to overworked, underpaid and therefore underqualified police officers." Quick continued, "Do I really want a man or woman who's worked 16 hours straight, with a gun in their hand, with state-sanctioned ability to take my life, who is tired—do I want that person authorized to police me? The answer to that is no."[20] The effects of maintaining a smaller force in Vallejo—both positive and clearly negative—should give policy makers pause.

When we ask evaluative questions rooted in the present (*What's working? What's not working?*), we inevitably discuss values. The interventions we implement to reform policing in the United States are all rooted in values. If we require police departments to diversify by focusing on the recruitment of Black and Hispanic officers, we're saying that we value diverse police departments and believe diversity will help solve some issues we see with the over- and under-policing of predominantly Black and Hispanic neighborhoods. If we require that police departments pair their officers with mental health professionals, we're saying that we value treating people experiencing homelessness or a mental health crisis as people who are in need of help, not as criminals.

3. What should be done next?

Once we've figured out what's happening and what's working (and what may not be working), the next logical question to ask is what now should be done to address the policy problem we identified:

> How could the City of Chicago best ensure that its residents' public safety needs are met as effectively as possible?

Asking questions about the future (*What should be done next?*) focuses attention on choices, which allows people of different political persuasions to arrive at a shared vision of what things could look like if they worked together. "If you want to make a joint decision," writes Jay Heinrichs in his book *Thank You for Arguing*, "you need to focus on the future. A future focus is what Aristotle saved for his favorite rhetoric. He called it "'deliberative,' because it argues about choices and helps us decide how to meet our mutual goals."[21] If focusing on the past risks leading to disagreements about who is to blame, and if focusing on the present can incite passionate arguments about good and bad, asking questions about the future forces people to make a joint decision dependent on particular circumstances informed by—but not dominated by—cold facts and indelible values. Once we can agree on the future we'd like to see, we can take deliberate steps to build that future. We can figure out a way to make it happen, together. "Most arguments," Heinrichs continues, "take place in the wrong tense. Choose the right tense. If you want your audience to make a choice, focus on the future."[22]

One group in Chicago thinking about the future along these lines is the Workers Center for Racial Justice, which has proposed a $900 million cut to the city's police budget, spread out over three years. According to its Proposal for Equitable Public Safety Reinvestment, about $700 million could be reinvested in housing, public health, and family and support services. The rest could be used to establish units like Denver's Crisis Intervention Response Units. These units would be staffed by traffic responders, crisis workers, mental health providers, and human services employees who are better equipped to respond to the calls for service that make up the bulk of 911 calls—and don't necessarily require police officers—such as traffic incidents, mental health crises, and the filing of crime incident reports. Such cuts, according to the proposal, would bring the city's per capita spending on policing "just under the current average spent among the nation's top ten most populous cities."[23]

CHAPTER 2

Mastering Deductive, Evaluative, and Prescriptive Policy Answers

Once we've figured out which questions we need to ask, the logical next step is to answer them. There are three types of policy answers that correspond to the three types of policy questions. In this chapter, I'm going to show you how to answer each type of question and discuss how the answer to each question, if answered well, leads to further questions that will need to be answered if you want to persuade your reader with your policy story.

THE THREE TYPES OF POLICY ANSWERS

To answer the three types of policy questions, we have three types of policy answers (table 2.1), which I call descriptive, evaluative, and prescriptive.

1. *Descriptive*: Answers the question "What's happening?"
2. *Evaluative*: Answers the question "What's working?"
3. *Prescriptive*: Answers the question "What should be done next?"

Let's look at these three types of policy answers in more detail.

1. Descriptive policy answers

For example: To what extent are women represented on US corporate boards of directors? This is clearly a "What's happening?" question, which means it needs a descriptive answer. Put simply, we're going to describe what is happening with the representation of women on US corporate boards—nothing more.

Over the last decade, women have increased their representation on US corporate boards to about 16 percent.

Asked and answered. Our work here is done, right? Actually, no; this is where the fun starts. Once we have an answer to the question, we need to think about what follow-up questions our readers will likely have for us. If we want to tell a persuasive policy story, we're going to need answers to questions like these as well:

- What is *supposed* to be happening? Is 16 percent too low? Too high? Just right?
- What factors may affect the number of women who sit on US corporate boards?
- What barriers, if any, may be preventing more women from serving?
- What policy options, if any, could be implemented to increase the representation of women on US corporate boards?
- What might happen next if nothing is done to address what's happening?

To determine what is *supposed* to be happening, we need criteria. It's not enough to point out an issue and expect your readers to agree that what you've found is problematic. To determine what should be happening, we can look to laws, regulations, contracts, grant agreements, internal control measures, industry best practices, expected performance measures, clearly defined business practices, and benchmarks—basically anything against which we can compare what's happening.

Other times, when there may not be accepted criteria to use, we can look to our readers for cues about what should be happening. If, for example, our readers are private sector executives, members of corporate boards, and company shareholders, we may want to ask what their goals are. What do they care about? Perhaps the goal should be to ensure that women represent the same percentage of corporate board seats as they represent in the overall population—about 51 percent. Or perhaps the goal should be to ensure that women represent the same percentage of corporate board seats as they represent in the respective company's customer base. Target's base shoppers, for example, are 60–63 percent women, on average, so perhaps 60 percent of Target's

TABLE 2.1. The three types of policy answers with examples

1. Descriptive
What do the data tell us? What's the policy problem you found?

What are the current trends in and status of marriage and labor force participation in American households?

The composition and work patterns of American households have changed dramatically over the past 50 years as fewer adults get married and more women work outside the home.

2. Evaluative
Which policy option, if any, has been shown to be more effective at addressing the policy problem?

How effective are programs designed to incentivize Americans to find and maintain work?

Programs designed to incentivize Americans who live below the poverty line have had mixed effects when it comes to increasing the total number of hours worked.

3. Prescriptive
What policy option could be implemented to address the policy problem—and why?

How could states help increase the number of workers who save money in a retirement account?

Expanding access to accounts offered by employers, enrolling workers in accounts automatically, and incentivizing workers to save have been shown to be effective state-led strategies in other developed countries.

corporate board should also be women (currently, women make up 36 percent of its board).

Or perhaps the readers care less about "optics" and "political acceptability" and more about effectiveness and financial performance. In that case, they may be interested to know that some research shows that having a broader range of perspectives represented on a diverse corporate board results in better decisions because the board members need to work harder to reach consensus.[1] Other research has found that boards with more women have a positive impact on their company's financial performance.[2] Your readers may be interested in taking steps to increase short-term profits, or they may be more concerned with ensuring long-term sustainability. It's our job to understand what our readers want and need (the focus of chapter 3). Once we know what they want and need, we can tailor the policy answers we provide to help our readers solve a problem and achieve their goals.

2. Evaluative policy answers

For example: How effective is the Choose to Change program in reducing arrests for violent crime among the program's participants? Any time you're trying to determine how effective something has been, you're going to need to give an evaluative answer that tells the reader what works, what doesn't, and why.

> Those who participated in Choose to Change had 48 percent fewer arrests for violent crimes than their peers who did not take part in it.

In 2015, two Chicago nonprofit groups developed Choose to Change to help prevent youth violence in the city. Choose to Change is a six-month intervention that connects participants with mentors who use trauma-informed cognitive behavioral therapy to help young people process trauma and develop a new set of decision-making skills.

To determine how effective the program was, the University of Chicago's Crime and Education Labs designed a randomized controlled trial to evaluate the program's impact on academic engagement and justice system involvement by comparing those who were selected by lottery to participate in the program with those who were not. In addition to showing a substantial reduction in the number of arrests for violent crime, the trial's preliminary results showed that participants in the program

- were 39 percent less likely to have been arrested for any offense compared with the control group,
- attended an additional seven days of school in the year after the program began (a 6 percent increase), and
- had 32 percent fewer misconduct incidents in school compared with their peers who did not take part.[3]

Readers won't be satisfied with this answer, however promising it seems to be. They may understandably have follow-up questions:

- How do we know the positive result is attributable to the program and not to some other variable or intervention?
- Why was the program so successful?
- How long after the program ends can we expect the benefits to last?
- Could Choose to Change work on a larger scale? Or in a different city?

All good questions, right? Any reasonable person trying to figure out how to reduce violence among Chicago's young people will surely want to know the answers to these questions and more. Our job, in turn, is to figure out what kinds of follow-up questions readers will probably have and to answer those too. If we do that, our policy story will be that much more responsive to readers and their needs, which will make it that much more convincing.

Luckily, we know many of the answers to the questions above. We know that the positive results can be attributed to the program because the researchers set up the gold standard of evaluation: a randomized controlled trial. Doing so allowed them to account for other differences that may have affected the outcomes being evaluated. Because they randomly assigned the young people to one group or the other, whatever differences existed among them should have balanced out, as long as there were enough young people who participated. The researchers were confident enough to conclude that the program caused the differences they had observed in the outcomes evaluated. This methodology isn't perfect, of course. There is no such thing as perfection in policy analysis. But it's the best tool we've got.

As for why the program was so successful, the secret seems to lie in positive effects from cognitive behavioral therapy. "The keys to the success of [Choose to Change] are teaching youth the cognitive behavioral skills needed to stop, think, and choose while providing a supportive mentoring relationship to practice these skills with the mentor and with other youth in the program," said Amanda Whitlock, senior vice president of behavioral health at Children's Home & Aid.[4]

But how long can we expect these positive effects to persist? "Typically, what we see with many evaluations of adolescent programming is that the positive benefits diminish as soon as programming ends," said Nour Abdul-Razzak, a postdoctoral fellow at the Crime and Education Labs. Not so with Choose to Change. Researchers found in their follow-up, which occurred two years after the first cohort had finished the program, that many of the positive outcomes had not diminished. "The fact that the impacts of [Choose to Change]," Abdul-Razzak said, "last even after the program ends is very encouraging, and speaks to the ability of the program to support a safer and brighter future for young people."[5]

Based on the promising preliminary outcomes published by the Crime and Education Labs, the City of Chicago and Chicago Public Schools expanded Choose to Change to serve even more young people. On February 21, 2020, Chicago's mayor announced that the city would fund an expansion of the program's reach over three years. "Our children are the future of Chicago and as a City, we have a fundamental obligation to ensure young people who are involved in gun violence have the resources and supports they need to get back on the right path, pursue their dreams and live a life free from violence," said Mayor Lori E. Lightfoot. "That is why through our landmark multi-year expansion of Choose to Change, we are not only investing in these young people, we are transforming their lives and shaping Chicago's future for the better."[6]

Could Choose to Change work in other cities, such as New York or Los Angeles? It's possible. The only way to find out for sure is to pilot the program, collect relevant data, analyze the data, and make adjustments to the program as necessary.

3. Prescriptive policy answers

For example: How could the Pension Benefit Guarantee Corporation better ensure the long-term sustainability of its business model and protect the retirement security of American workers? Whenever you're thinking about what *could* or *should* be done next to solve a policy problem, you're going to need a prescriptive policy story that tells the reader what needs to be done and why.

> The Pension Benefit Guarantee Corporation should revise how it charges premiums to better reflect the risk posed by private companies' pension plans.

I don't expect you to have heard of the Pension Benefit Guarantee Corporation (PBGC). I had never heard of it until I was asked in 2011 to assist a team of researchers in writing a report that would help the officials who oversaw PBGC's single-employer insurance plan pull themselves out of a $26 billion hole.

PBGC was established in 1974 under the Employee Retirement Income Security Act, and its mission from the start has been to protect the pension benefits of American private sector workers by charging insurance premiums to companies that offer pension benefits to their employees. If a company were to go out of business, PBGC would take over the company's pension plan and use the money it had collected to continue paying the benefits. By 2011, however, PBGC was in dire financial straits. That year PBGC collected $2.1 billion in premiums to insure the benefits of 44 million workers, retirees, and beneficiaries, but PBGC paid out $5.5 billion in benefits. It doesn't take a math whiz to figure out PBGC had a real problem on its hands. PBGC was hemorrhaging money, with no relief in sight.

The next question we had to ask was *why*? Why was PBGC paying out so much more than it was taking in? It turns out that since PBGC's inception, the premiums it charged employers did not accurately reflect the risks that PBGC insures against, namely, the risk of an employer with an underfunded pension plan filing for bankruptcy and triggering the need for PBGC to take responsibility for paying its benefits. Instead, PBGC generally charged a flat-rate premium based on the number of people covered by an employer's pension plan.

Why didn't PBGC adjust the way it factored in risk when determining how much to charge employers? PBGC could, for example, factor in the employer's overall financial strength. PBGC could also evaluate the employer's investment strategy. When we asked PBGC that question, the officials that oversee it said they were afraid they'd put an undue burden on employers if they raised premiums. Think about that for a second. What they were telling us was that they were going to go out of business relatively slowly rather than risk going out of business more quickly. That was the primary reason they were going out of business and jeopardizing the retirement security of millions of Americans— they were too averse to risk.

To help solve PBGC's financial problems, we had to figure out what questions PBGC had that it needed answers to. After learning about the aversion to raising premiums, we decided that what PBGC's officials needed to know was whether their fears were warranted. In other words, what would happen if PBGC raised its premiums? Would that cause employers with underfunded pensions to file for bankruptcy and hasten the implosion of PBGC? To answer that important question, some wicked-smart data scientists at the US Government Accountability Office developed a predictive model from a data sample of about 2,700 pension plans to analyze the potential effects of different premium structures. Under one structure, employers that were relatively financially healthy would pay less while relatively financially risky employers would pay more.

We then took the model and shared its findings with several retirement experts to get their take on it. They initially echoed PBGC's concern that higher premiums would lead employers to terminate their pension plans, but they suggested that if PBGC capped premiums and averaged employers' pension funding levels over multiple years to reduce volatility, an updated premium structure incorporating relevant risk factors could help PBGC reduce its deficit. Prior analyses conducted by the Government Accountability Office and others had shown that employers file for bankruptcy and terminate their pension plans because of other factors, such as the size of the employer, whether its employees could collectively bargain, and the overall costs of the employer's pension plan; these factors are more important than the cost of premiums. Unless PBGC incorporated relevant risk factors when determining how much it charged in premiums, we concluded, it risked destroying the retirement security for millions of Americans.

As with descriptive and evaluative policy answers, prescriptive policy answers will lead to more questions that need to be answered if you expect your readers to be persuaded by your policy recommendations. Questions like these:

- How exactly will the prescribed policy recommendation address the identified policy challenge?
- Why is the prescribed policy recommendation better than alternative steps that could be taken?
- How will we know if the prescribed policy recommendation is effective in addressing the identified policy challenge?

In July 2012, eight months after the Government Accountability Office had published its report, Congress approved premium increases to better reflect the risk posed to PBGC by certain pension plans. Congress did so again in December 2013 and again in November 2015. PBGC also proposed two policy options to help prevent hardships for small employers with a higher default risk that might result from higher risk-based premiums. First, PBGC wanted to have a phase-in period to allow enough time for employers to improve the funding status of their pension plan and to prepare for the premium increase. Second, PBGC wanted to create a premium cap for smaller companies.[7]

In November 2019, PBGC noted in its annual report for fiscal year 2019 that its single-employer program had a budget surplus of $8.7 billion. In eight short years, the corporation went from a $26 billion deficit to having almost $9 billion left over at the end of the year. The turnaround happened all because the corporation had implemented a risk-based premium structure.[8]

We figured out what questions PBGC needed answers to. We answered them. PBGC took our answers and solved a problem. Solving that problem had a positive impact on millions of Americans. In short, we helped change the world.

CHAPTER 3

Meeting the Unique Needs of Your Reader

One of the primary reasons why many policy analysts struggle to write clearly and concisely is that they don't have clarity about whom they're writing for. Before you analyze your data, you've got to get a clear understanding of who your readers are, what they want to achieve, and how you can help them achieve it. To figure out what your readers need, you can ask yourself six questions—the answers to which will help you know what research questions to ask, what kinds of data to collect and analyze, and how to communicate the results of your analysis in an interesting and persuasive way.

1. What are the readers' goals?

This is a *really* important question—perhaps the most important. Think about it this way: What do your readers need to know to help them achieve their goals and accomplish their mission? If you want your writing to be valuable to your readers, you need to position what you write as a helpful tool that readers can use to get what they want.

For example, imagine you're a policy analyst working for a politician who needs to decide whether to support a new bill or oppose it. The question we must ask ourselves is, What information does this person need to make an informed decision? One goal of politicians, of course, is—or should be—to do what's right for their constituents. But they may also need to factor in how different special interests may respond to their vote and how donors may feel about it. At the end of the day, most politicians want to stay in office. That's their primary goal. And to stay in office, they need money, which can be harder to get if you annoy the people who have a lot of it.

That's not to say, though, that there's no way to persuade a politician to take a stand unpopular with moneyed interests. Plenty of politicians at the national level in the United States have declared they will no longer take donations from lobbyists and political action campaigns. Still, that doesn't change the fact they need money, so one goal of these politicians may be to energize the base of small donors who can give them enough money to stay in office. In any event, if you the policy analyst do not account for the reader's interests and goals in your analysis and recommendations, I highly doubt you are going to persuade them.

Positioning yourself as a useful advisor in this way isn't as easy as it may sound. Humans are not always "internally consistent" and "logically coherent," to borrow from the lexicon of the Chicago School of Economics. In addition to being susceptible to inaccurate assumptions and misleading biases, the way that human brains perceive reality largely depends on circumstance and our relation to the people around us. Many experiments with small groups have shown that what each of us understands to be acceptable—and what we consider to be the "truth"—is defined through our interactions with people close to us physically, ideologically, emotionally, and aesthetically. When the people close to us believe something to be true, that group belief becomes, for each of us, a factual reality.[1]

Evidence of how our relations affect our perceptions were on full display in the United States after the coronavirus pandemic struck. Using a wealth of micro-level data, researchers at the University of Chicago used machine learning and a novel quasi-experimental design to study how partisanship influenced the use of face masks to thwart the spread of the coronavirus. At the end of July 2020, they published a working paper in which they shared their findings:

1. Face mask use is robustly correlated with partisanship, meaning that Democratic voters were more likely to support face mask mandates and Republican voters were more likely to oppose them.

2. The impact of partisanship has not been offset by local policy interventions, meaning that when a mayor or governor mandates

the use of face masks, such interventions are not strong enough to overcome the politically driven decision whether to support mask use.

3. Partisanship is the single most important predictor of mask use, not COVID-19 severity or local policies.

"These results," the researchers conclude, "unmask how partisanship undermines effective public responses to collective risk and how messaging by political agents can increase public engagement with mask use."[2]

On top of whatever influence our circumstances and relationships have on us, human perceptions also depend on whatever worldview we ascribe to. Your stance on various public policy issues likely hinges on your economic, ethical, religious, legal, and civic worldview, which you have used throughout your life to bring coherence to an extremely complicated world. Whether you support social service programs that benefit people experiencing homelessness, for example, may depend on whether you see yourself as a free-market capitalist or a social democrat, or it may depend on how literally you interpret religious doctrine. Your stance on the legalization of marijuana, similarly, may depend on how much you identify as a libertarian or on your views related to medical ethics. The process by which we all make decisions is, therefore, messy and imperfect, and the decisions we make or the way we perceive the world is not always rational or easy to predict.

2. What do the readers already know?

If you're writing for readers with expertise in your subject area, you won't need to spend a lot of time explaining the background of an issue or the history of a policy challenge. No readers want to commission a report that's full of information they already know. On the other hand, if you're writing for readers with little knowledge of your topic and little understanding of statistics, you must spend time informing them about the topic and explaining how you arrived at your conclusions from your data analysis.

Keep in mind, though, that even seemingly simple information may be difficult to process since many Americans are not "proficiently literate." In 2017, the National Center for Education Statistics reported that 51 percent of American adults (aged 16–65 years) scored "below proficient" on a literacy test that measured their ability to "understand, use, and respond appropriately" to written documents. The study, conducted by the Program for the International Assessment of Adult Competencies, was designed to assess nationally representative samples of people from 38 countries around the world on a broad range of abilities needed to succeed in the twenty-first-century economy. The average score for US participants—on a scale of 0–500—was 272, only 5 points above the international average. The average adult in Japan scored 296, the highest score of any country.

In terms of "basic mathematical and computational skills," also known as numeracy, 62 percent of American adults scored below proficient, despite having some of the highest levels of educational attainment. The international average score for numeracy was 263. The average score in the United States was 6 points below that average and 31 points below the average adult in Japan.

Finally, in "digital problem solving," 64 percent of American adults scored below proficient in assessing and interpreting "information in digital environments to perform practical tasks." With a score of 274 out of 500, the average American again scored below the international average of 278 points. The average adult in Japan earned the highest score, 20 points higher than adults in the United States.[3]

I would bet that most people who would score below proficient are not big consumers of policy writing. They are probably educated but may not understand statistics. A good example of this comes from an August 2020 interview that President Donald Trump had with an Axios national political correspondent, Jonathan Swan. When discussing the Trump administration's handling of the coronavirus pandemic, Swan said that one of the statistics he found alarming was the number of Americans who were dying each day. The president responded by pulling out loose sheets of paper, each with a graphic. "Let's look at death," he said, thumbing through the papers. "Right here," he said, pointing. "The United States is lowest in numerous categories. We're lower than the world. Lower than Europe." He then handed one of the graphics to Swan.

While Swan scrutinized it with a furrowed brow, the president flipped to another page, this one with four colorful bars: "Here's case death." As Philip Bump reported in the *Washington Post* the day after the interview aired, cases of coronavirus were surging in southern and western states, although the number of people who died after contracting the virus (as a percentage of those infected) was going down. "So," Bump writes, "the administration began focusing on the ratio between those two metrics since it made the United States seem as if it was faring particularly well. If one country has 100 new cases and five deaths a day, its mortality rate is 5 percent. If the United States has 100,000 new cases and 1,000 deaths, its mortality rate is only 1 percent. Ergo: a success!"[4]

"Oh," Swan interrupted. "You're doing death as a proportion of cases. I'm talking about death as a proportion of population. That's where the US is *really* bad. Much worse than South Korea, Germany, etc."

"You can't do that," the president responded, "You have to . . . You have to go by where . . . Look," he stammered, flipping again to the colorful bar chart. "This is the United States. You have to go by the cases. What it says is when you have somebody where there's a case, the people that live from those cases."

What the president failed to realize, or at least refused to admit, was that preventing someone infected with the coronavirus from dying does not mean the virus is under control. "It's surely a relevant statistic," Swan pushed back, "to say that if the US has X population and X percentage of death of that population versus South Korea—" The president interrupted, again insisting on his statistics. Swan redirected. "Look at South Korea, for example," he said. "Fifty-one million population, three hundred deaths. It's crazy compared to America."[5] What does all this mean? It means that we as policy analysts and writers must work *that* much harder to translate statistical data and jargon into the simplest language possible.

Our reader's literacy, numeracy, and digital problem-solving skills are further complicated by the ways the human brain processes information. Our brains have two systems of thinking—known as System 1 and System 2 in the parlance of Nobel Prize–winning economist Daniel Kahneman—and these two systems fight for control of our thoughts and behaviors. System 1 operates automatically and involuntarily. System 2 operates consciously. Because all human brains are inherently lazy, in that they want to conserve energy, we rely on System 1 whenever we face a relatively simple problem because System 1 is more energy efficient. When we are confronted with a more difficult or novel problem, however, System 1 generally calls on System 2 to analyze the available evidence and arrive at a logical conclusion. Sometimes, though, our brains do not accurately perceive how difficult a problem is, and we place too much trust in System 1 to solve it.[6]

This becomes a problem when System 1 activates assumptions or biases that are inaccurate or irrelevant. Take, for example, a phenomenon known as *cognitive ease*, which happens because things that are quicker to decipher or more familiar to us also seem truer to us than things that are unusual or difficult to interpret. Another bias that policy analysts need to be aware of is *confirmation bias*, which describes the human tendency to search for and find confirming evidence for a preexisting belief while simultaneously overlooking examples that refute it.

3. What keeps the readers up at night?

What are your readers afraid of? What challenges may they be facing that they're not being forthright about? One way to find out is to ask them such questions. Another way to approach this is to read the stories your readers tell about themselves and compare those with the stories the popular press and various think tanks write about them.

This is something I did when I worked for the federal government. When we were tasked with evaluating a federal program or a process within a federal agency, I would do a Google search to see what the agency's public relations team was saying about the agency's work. I was checking for any disconnect between what the agency was saying and what others were saying about it. If there was a disconnect, I'd dig a little deeper. Usually there was some kind of scandal or executive-level wrongdoing or mismanagement. Sometimes it was as simple as the head of the program being replaced or the agency requesting more funding than it received.

When I worked on engagements for the Department of Veterans Affairs, it was easy to see how badly the media was beating up the department all the time. The news reported scandal after scandal. To position ourselves as helpful—and therefore more valuable to the department—we'd dig deeper into what was contributing to these scandals. Did the department get new leadership? Was there a budget issue? Were there new regulations its employees had to follow or requirements they had to meet? Did the department have the staffing and the resources needed to fulfill its mission? The degree to which our recommendations for improvement were valuable to our readers depended on how clearly we showed them we were there to *help* them solve their problems, not to beat up on them for having problems.

4. What have the readers tried in the past? How did it work out?

Just because something has been tried in the past doesn't mean that it can't be tried again. Political circumstances change. Public opinion changes. Factors on the ground change. The world in 2020 looked nothing like the world before the coronavirus pandemic. After passing the largest stimulus bill in American history—amounting to $2.4 trillion—the idea of spending trillions of dollars on universal health care and universal basic income didn't seem so far-fetched. Calls to abolish the carceral state and redirect the billions of dollars spent on police grew louder and louder.

We as policy analysts need to know how we got here, what's been tried before, what happened, why it happened that way, and whether anything different about the circumstances today might lead to a different outcome. We never want to get caught flat-footed by presenting a policy solution that our readers already tried and saw fail and that we knew nothing about. Even if none of the information we've gathered about the readers makes it into our report, getting a better sense of what our readers know and think can inform the editorial decisions that make our writing matter more than it would have otherwise.

5. How averse to risk are the readers?

If you're writing for readers who are more innovative—think Silicon Valley's "fail fast and break things" mentality—where risk is viewed as necessary and desirable, you can probably feel more comfortable making policy recommendations that are a little risky. If, on the other hand, you're writing for a governmental organization or a nonprofit that abhors risk, then you must make recommendations fit for caution.

My colleagues and I at the Government Accountability Office used to joke that the readers for most of our reports were the kind who didn't want to be the first one to think of an idea. They wanted to be the seventh or eighth person to have the idea because it took that long for the stars to align, so to speak. The first or second person to have the idea, it seemed, would either be ignored or run out on a rail, as my grandfather used to say.

What if you want to recommend something important but risky, yet you're convinced your readers won't be up for doing the right thing because it's too hard? I'm not telling you to always play it safe or to tell your readers only what they want to hear. Some things are worth going out on a limb for. What I want you to understand, though, is that if you're going to go out on a limb and recommend that risk-averse readers do something risky, then you've got to tell them an interesting and persuasive story that gives them what they need to take that leap of faith. Nobody said this was going to be easy.

Another thing to keep in mind is that you might not have a totally clear picture of your readers' level of risk aversion. They may tell you they are less averse to risk than they really are. Or they may seem averse because they haven't yet found the right thing to take a risk on. This too is part of the analyst's job—if you want to write something that matters.

6. What barriers do the readers face?

You can write an incredibly persuasive report based on robust data and impressive analysis, but if there is some challenge or barrier that will stop the readers from listening and taking the steps you suggest, then you are probably wasting your time and theirs. You absolutely must know if there is anything that can stand in your readers' way. If you are writing to the head of a government program that isn't performing as effectively as it should, you've got to inquire about certain things. Does the program have the leadership it needs? Does it have the money and resources? The expertise, the staffing, the political will? If the readers listen to you and do what you suggest they should, what sorts of unintended consequences could they face? Do you have a plan to help them with that?

Again, I'm not telling you to pull back or muzzle yourself. Sometimes we are going to write reports we know will not result in the change we think needs to be made. At least not yet. Just remember that sometimes when you're contributing a policy report to the conversation on some topic, you're not just talking to the powers that be. You're also talking to your peers and those who follow. You may be laying the groundwork for something special—even when it doesn't feel that way—with every word you write.

You may also be wondering when you should ask these questions about the readers. At the beginning? At the end? During data collection? The short answer: yes. You should ask these questions from the beginning, through data collection and analysis, all while you're writing and revising, and even in the final seconds before you hit "send." Do not think of them as a checklist of items to tick off and be done with. Instead, think of them as questions to revisit continually. And use the answers to refine your approach, as appropriate.

CHAPTER 4

Developing Stronger Policy Recommendations Using Human-Centered Design

In this chapter, we're going to explore several human-centered design tools that anyone can use to collect, analyze, and synthesize data, and I'll then illustrate how you can use human-centered design to develop sound policy recommendations that address the root cause of policy challenges without losing sight of the people who will be affected by your work.

I've found the best way to teach this material is to introduce a case study, so in this chapter we are discussing the Emergency Food Security Program, which the US Congress authorized in 2016 under the Global Food Security Act to provide assistance to people experiencing food insecurity around the world in the form of cash transfers and food vouchers. This was an important development considering that from 1954, when the Agricultural Trade Development and Assistance Act was signed into law, until the Obama administration, the United States had provided food aid through the Food for Peace program only in the form of agricultural commodities (e.g., wheat, corn, oats, rye, soybeans, sugarcane, and grain sorghum) that US farmers grew and that US-flagged ships transported overseas. This type of aid is known as *in-kind* food aid. The original goals of Food for Peace were to (1) divest the United States of accumulated agricultural surpluses, (2) improve the domestic food market, and (3) stimulate new food markets overseas.[1]

Beginning in 2010, the US Agency for International Development (USAID) offered what it termed "market-based food assistance" to help alleviate hunger and improve food security around the world. How it worked in practice was USAID granted funds to humanitarian organizations in the United States and abroad with which they could purchase locally or regionally sourced food within an affected area or could distribute cash transfers for food or food vouchers to those most in need. These market-based approaches were intended to complement in-kind food assistance, and by 2016 they were formally authorized under the Emergency Food Security Program.[2]

The explicit purpose of the Emergency Food Security Program, according to a 2018 overview of US international food assistance published by the Congressional Research Service, is to provide cash aid when in-kind aid could not "arrive soon enough or could potentially disrupt local markets or when it is unsafe to operate in conflict zones."[3] The fact that the United States long provided only in-kind food aid had, it turns out, become a point of contention for many involved in humanitarian assistance.

By the time President Barack Obama took office in 2008, several rigorous studies had shown that it was more expensive to ship food from the United States on US-flagged ships than it was to provide cash benefits or food vouchers, and in-kind food aid also took much longer to deliver. In 2013, for example, three economists published the results of a study that showed buying food locally or distributing cash or vouchers resulted in a time savings of nearly 14 weeks (a 62 percent gain). They also found that buying grains locally saved more than 50 percent, on average, whereas buying processed commodities was not always cost-effective. To generate these estimates, the economists compared local and regional procurement activities in nine countries against transoceanic in-kind shipments from the United States to the same nine countries during the same time frame. The economists concluded that where markets can adequately meet increased demand for food through local and regional procurement, doing so can often yield valuable cost and time savings, which may allow donors to reach more recipients faster.[4] By 2017, USAID granted, for the first time, more money for cash transfer and food voucher programs that it did for in-kind food donations.[5]

The creation of the Emergency Food Security Program may seem like a simple solution to a straightforward policy challenge. If, however, you dig a little deeper into the politics surrounding this issue (which we will do below), you may be surprised by how complex it is.

WHAT IS HUMAN-CENTERED DESIGN?

"Everyone designs," Herbert A. Simon once said, "who devises courses of action aimed at changing existing situations into preferred ones." Herb Simon was awarded the Nobel Prize in economics in 1978. His primary research interest was how organizations make decisions, and he was best known for his theories of "bonded rationality" and "satisficing." I came across Simon's quote in a human-centered design certification course I took. Human-centered design, according to the LUMA Institute, is a way of solving problems that focuses on people above other factors. Human-centered designers, in other words, collect data, figure out what people need, and develop solutions to meet those needs by using a variety of brainstorming, analysis, and communication strategies.

To begin, let's imagine the policy question we want to answer:

How could the United States plan to respond to future international food emergencies so that people facing food insecurity receive timely, cost-effective, and appropriate assistance?

To answer this question, we must first figure out what is happening. What we want to happen, as expressed in the question, is for USAID food assistance to be timely, cost-effective, and appropriate for the conditions in the affected area. If we find a gap between what is happening and what we want to happen, we then must determine what's causing that gap. It will be important for us to evaluate cash transfers and food voucher programs to see if they are more timely, cost-effective, and appropriate than in-kind food assistance. If they are better in all those ways, we'll want to figure out whether there are any specific conditions that need to be present. Only after we feel confident about our research into all those concerns can we answer the prescriptive question that started this line of inquiry.

THE FIRST STEP IN HUMAN-CENTERED DESIGN: LOOKING

I'd bet that when you think about the word *research*, you probably think of academic literature, case studies, government reports, and maybe even reputable media coverage. And you wouldn't be wrong. If you want to understand what is happening in a specific policy area, you've got to start with what other people have thought about the topic and what previous studies have already found. But this isn't always what policy analysts do. Many focus instead on databases and plotting out how they might use some calculation they learned in graduate school to make sense of all those ones and zeroes.

Even those who realize they must review mountains of qualitative political and macro-organization theory before they'll likely be able to contribute something new and useful to a policy discussion can sometimes end up buried, always searching for another book to read, another white paper to digest, another model to dissect. The research you *could* do on any given policy challenge would likely fill a small library and occupy you for months, if not years. Attempting to read everything that's ever been written about your topic might be admirable, but it would also be misguided. Insights do not emerge without some strategy. You must be strategic in your exploration of the literature.

One way to bring purpose to your research is to start with the people affected by the policy challenge you're investigating. Once you've got a better sense of what the people on the ground are thinking, feeling, and experiencing, you can be more strategic in your research. Think of this process like how an ethnographer might. First, we must observe, and then we can try to make sense of what we see—not necessarily the other way around. Human-centered designers observe people using some combination of three techniques: (1) interviews, (2) fly-on-the-wall observations, and (3) contextual inquiries.

Interviewing

It's been my experience that most people enjoy telling stories about themselves, the work they do, the challenges they face, and how they have coped with life's setbacks. A good interview can help you understand things about a policy problem that data may not: how people feel about things, what they want, what barriers stop them from getting what they want, why certain problems are occurring, and what opinions they may hold but don't always express. I love interviewing people, mostly because I think it challenges my own preconceptions and deepens my empathy for people I may not know much about. Having interesting findings from interviews can also build credibility with stakeholders because you went to the front line of the problem rather than hole yourself up in your office running regression analyses.

Fly-on-the-wall observations

In addition to interviewing people, you can observe people (without interfering) and *see* what they know and do. When people do not think they are being observed, they say and do things they're not necessarily aware of or would think to account for. What shortcuts do people take? What processes are in place but never used? Is there something one person does that feels more innovative or effective than what everyone else is doing?

Contextual inquiry

If interviewing people lets us hear what people say and observing them shows us what people do, contextual inquiry can help us understand what people say they do. To paraphrase the influential anthropologist Margaret Mead, these three things are usually entirely different. A contextual inquiry places you in the midst of a person's environment and affords you an opportunity to ask questions about their experiences in context as they are happening. Input comes directly from the people who have the most knowledge, saving you from making wrong inferences about how and why things are done.

How can these strategies be applied?

Thanks to some interesting investigative work the Government Accountability Office (GAO) did on USAID's food assistance programs, we know that USAID has a limited ability to assess the overall performance (i.e., timeliness, cost-effectiveness, and appropriateness) of cash transfer and food voucher projects relative to in-kind food aid. In 2016, GAO reported that USAID and the partners it works with overseas to implement food aid programs had developed a plan to monitor cash transfer and food voucher projects that included (1) verifying information provided by implementing partners through a variety of mechanisms; (2) surveying implementing partners to gather information on the relevance, efficiency, and effectiveness of the assistance; and (3) visiting distribution sites regularly to speak with beneficiaries and retailers about their experiences.[6]

When GAO analysts reviewed the evaluation reports that USAID's implementing partners had prepared, they found that many of them lacked required data. Only one of the fourteen reports the analysts reviewed included all the data the implementing partners were required to collect. In addition, GAO analysts found that the indicators USAID was using to measure the timeliness, cost-effectiveness, and appropriateness of cash transfers and food vouchers were flawed in fundamental ways. For example, the indicator USAID used to track the timeliness of the assistance it provided did not compare how long it was scheduled to take with how long it actually took, meaning that USAID had no idea whether its assistance was being distributed without delays. The indicators USAID used for cost-effectiveness and appropriateness were equally flawed.[7]

We could say, therefore, that there is no way to know how timely, cost-effective, and appropriate cash transfers and food vouchers are compared with in-kind food donations because we do not have good data to tell us. Or we could interview agency officials and implementing partners to find out why the reports were not submitted in accordance with the requirements. We could also interview retailers and aid recipients to find out how long these processes took, in their experience, and how appropriate they were for their specific situations. Were they given money but had no place to spend it? Were they given food that was not culturally appropriate or easy to prepare?

We could then conduct site visits of our own and observe or perform contextual inquiries to see what people do and what they say they do when distributing aid and collecting and reporting data. The same goes for after the aid is distributed. What do people do with it? Do people try to sell the food they receive on a secondary market or use the cash payments for something other than food? Do armed insurgents commandeer the aid?

Finding answers to these sorts of questions with qualitative data could give us great insights into how we might answer our policy question—especially when the quantitative data we have leaves much to be desired.

THE SECOND STEP IN HUMAN-CENTERED DESIGN: UNDERSTANDING

Once we've collected a fair amount of quantitative and qualitative data, the next step we must take is understanding the data. One exercise I like to start this phase with is known in the human-centered design world as stakeholder mapping.

Stakeholder mapping

Accounting for the entire landscape of stakeholders can sometimes help us discover policy opportunities that were previously obscured for whatever reason. Seeing the policy issue as a system of interconnected actors can serve to reorient your approach or even lead to a redefinition of the question you're trying to answer or the problem you're trying to solve. When we put people at the center of an investigation, we can ask questions like these about them: (1) How are they affected by present policy? (2) What do they care about? (3) How much influence or power do they have? (4) What barriers do they face? (5) What steps have they taken recently to address the problems we found during the looking phase? (6) How do they stand to gain or lose if our preferred change to policy gets implemented?

To make the most of the exercise, it's best to convene a diverse team of collaborators to generate a comprehensive set of stakeholders. For each stakeholder your team identifies, briefly summarize their mindset by answering the questions in the preceding paragraph. Once your team has identified as many stakeholders as possible, draw lines with arrows connecting them. You should also label the lines to describe the relationships so that you don't forget them. (Using a whiteboard or a digital equivalent works well for this exercise.) Once you've completed the exercise, document your findings and return to them throughout the rest of your research to make sure that your policy story still aligns with what you know about the stakeholders.

When it comes to international food aid, there are plenty of stakeholders we need to consider. In addition to USAID specifically and the US Department of Agriculture generally, there are various nonprofit humanitarian assistance organizations that receive grant funds from USAID—organizations like Mercy Corps and Catholic Relief Services. Then there are the implementing partners on the ground and the people who receive the assistance. We also cannot forget the American farmers who grow and sell the crops USAID ships overseas. You'll find that the farmers, their political associations (such as National Association of Wheat Growers), and the commodity-purchasing companies that buy the farmers' crops have *plenty* of political pull in Washington, DC. So do the shipping companies and their lobbyists. There are a couple billion dollars a year to be made growing crops, selling them to the federal government, shipping them overseas, and donating them to people experiencing food insecurity.

These sorts of moneyed interests also like to point out that there are economic benefits to exporting American agricultural products and that, instead of sending cash or food vouchers, the United States should send *more* food. In 2018, according to the International Food Policy Research Institute, agricultural exports generated an additional $261 billion in economic activity in the United States, resulting in a total increase in economic output of $401 billion produced by about 1.2 million full-time US workers.[8]

There are also more practical reasons to choose in-kind food aid over cash transfers and food vouchers, according to Bob Stallman, former president of the American Farm Bureau Federation. "The problem with switching to cash donations is that cash too easily can be used for purposes other than feeding people," he wrote in 2013. "Food can only be useful going into someone's stomach. Shipping a cargo load of food, rather than the money to buy food (if it is available), is the best and most secure way to ensure that taxpayer-funded international food assistance actually makes it to hungry people overseas. Without that certainty, the full impact of our nation's donations could be easily slashed by administrative costs assessed by cooperating entities, or worse, siphoned off by inept or corrupt governments in recipient nations. That is why several international food aid organizations also oppose switching to cash donations."[9]

Others are quick to point out, however, that it isn't accurate to say that all food ends up in the bellies of hungry people. In July 2012, Claire Provost, writing for the *Guardian*, reported that the United States donates some food to nongovernmental organizations (NGOs) that then sell, or "monetize," that food in local markets to generate funds that can be used for other sorts of development programs. "Critics say this is an extremely inefficient way to raise funds for development," Provost writes, "as U.S. crops are more expensive to buy than those on offer in local markets, so NGOs are forced to sell them at below the cost of production."[10]

Aid workers, human rights observers, and journalists have also spoken up about the potential for in-kind food aid to *promote* conflict in certain situations. Specifically, they say that

- armed factions and opposition groups can easily appropriate humanitarian aid, which is often transported over long distances through territories only weakly controlled by the recipient government (with as much as 80 percent of aid being stolen during transport);
- even after food aid reaches the intended recipients, armed groups can easily confiscate it for their own purposes; and
- it is difficult to exclude members of local militia groups from being direct recipients if they are also malnourished.[11]

In a 2014 study published by the *American Economic Review*, Nathan Nunn and Nancy Qian validated these anecdotal observations by showing that an increase in US food aid increases the incidence and duration of civil conflicts—especially in countries with a recent history of civil conflict.[12]

What about the elected officials and the congressional committees in charge of matters related to agriculture and shipping? What do they have to say? In 2017, then chair of the Senate Foreign Relations Committee, Bob Corker of Tennessee (who retired in 2019), launched a campaign to reduce donations of in-kind food and increase the use of cash transfers and food vouchers. Corker also called for putting an end both to the cargo preference law requiring that 50 percent of US food aid be shipped on American vessels staffed by American merchant mariners and to the practice of monetization described above. Getting rid of "these utterly ridiculous requirements," as Corker called them, would free up, in his estimation, more than $300 million in US tax money that could feed 9.5 million more people each year.[13]

One thing you'll notice during this step in the process is that the balance of any policy ecosystem is defined by the interrelationships of its parts. Each stakeholder, whether key or peripheral, plays a role in how the system works. As a visualization of people's relationships, interactions, and needs, a stakeholder map can help us understand the extent and potential impact of our policy decisions.

Affinity clustering

Once you've got a better sense of who the key players are and how a change in policy will probably affect them, you can organize your data using a technique called affinity clustering. It's simple. All you do is sort the data you've collected into logical groups based on perceived similarity. The goal is to detect patterns by defining commonalities that are inherent but not necessarily obvious. In this way you'll gain insights into what might otherwise seem like disparate pieces of information.

To begin, gather the data you've collected and record each item on a sticky note. Form a team of collaborators and select one person to act as a facilitator. Then pick one person to take a piece of data—summarized on a sticky note—describe it and place it on the wall. Invite another person to do the same. Whenever a note summarizes evidence that complements a piece of evidence already posted, place it in the same area. If it's different, place it in its own area. Repeat this until all of the data have been placed on the wall. During this process, team members should question and challenge, suggesting when data should be regrouped.

Once your team is satisfied with the groupings, you can label them and begin discussing whether any of the data can be set aside (at least for now) because the data no longer fit into the story. Your team can also discuss which data are most persuasive and whether there are any holes in the story that still need to be filled.

I've done affinity clustering with dozens of research teams over the past decade. One trick I've used to speed this process up, and to make the categories of information easier to differentiate, is to organize the data into one of four elements of a policy story: (1) condition, (2) criteria, (3) cause, and (4) effect (table 4.1).

While not every policy story will require all four elements, all evaluative or prescriptive stories that lead to a policy recommendation absolutely will need all four, as you'll see in the discussion below.

TABLE 4.1. The four elements of a policy story

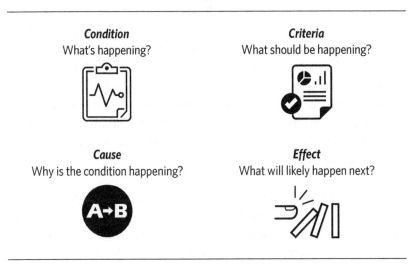

1. Condition: Answers the question "What's happening?"

The condition identifies "what is" and describes the circumstances that have been observed and documented while you were researching and collecting data. All policy stories should describe what is happening because—and I *cannot* stress this enough—it is imperative that we document, explain, compare, and negotiate our subjective perceptions of the world if we are to communicate with others—especially those who don't see the world the same way we do. Policy analysis and communication depend on a sense of shared reality: an ability to say that certain things are happening and that certain words can accurately describe what those things are.

The enemy of truth seeking in public policy is not the subjective nature of inquiry; it's losing the conditions in which discourse and debate and dialogue can occur constructively. "We know from experience that no one can adequately grasp the objective world in its full reality all on his own," writes influential philosopher and political theorist Hannah Arendt,

> because the world always shows and reveals itself to him from only one perspective, which corresponds to his standpoint in the world and is determined by it. If someone wants to see and experience the world as it "really" is, he can do so only by understanding it as something that is shared by many people, lies between them, showing itself differently to each and comprehensible only to the extent that many people can talk *about* it and exchange their opinions and perspectives with one another, over against one another. Only in the freedom of our speaking with one another does the world, as that about which we speak, emerge in its objectivity from all sides. Living in a real world and speaking with one another about it are basically one and the same.[14]

Sometimes the condition—the way something "really is"—will be something positive or desirable, and other times the condition will not be ideal. In such cases, we call that finding a *deficiency*. If you find a deficiency, your reader will want to know why you believe it's a deficiency and what you propose to fix it.

2. Criteria: Answers the question "What should be happening?"

It's not enough to point out a policy challenge and say it's a deficiency. To determine what should be happening, you need criteria that provide a context for understanding what you found. According to GAGAS, the generally accepted government auditing standards, which were developed by GAO, we can find criteria in "laws, regulations, contracts, grant agreements, standards, measures, expected performance, defined business practices, and benchmarks against which performance is compared or evaluated." In essence, "criteria identify the required or desired state or expectation with respect to the program or operation" and "provide a context for evaluating evidence and understanding the findings, conclusions, and recommendations."[15] The criteria you select, whether "GAGAS approved" or based on your readers' goals and needs, should be reasonable, attainable, and relevant to the matters being analyzed. Above all else, remember that policy analysis requires choice, and choice requires criteria based on preferences.

3. Cause: Answers the question "Why is the condition happening?"

There is another way to phrase the third question: What is causing the disparity between the condition and the criteria? I know what you might be thinking. Establishing causality sets a *high* bar to clear; are we supposed to make policy recommendations only when a cause-and-effect relationship has been established? No, of course not. When I talk about cause and effect in this chapter, it's nothing more than shorthand. If it helps, you can think in terms of *association* or *contributing factors* or *correlation*, depending on the study design, method, and results you use in your work.

I would bet that most readers of public policy don't have a nuanced understanding of the language we use to communicate cause and effect. I see this all the time—where a reader misinterprets or over-interprets causal inference findings. The fault can lie in several places, but we can trace at least part of the problem to an overly casual use of causal language. That doesn't mean we should never use causal language. Instead, we need to explain what the causal language we use means. Once we do that, we can make a clearer case for why the policy solution we propose will probably address the challenge we identified in the condition. If our proposed solution does not address the *cause* of a problem, our policy story will not persuade our readers to act.

This is also the point in your analysis where it may help to include some qualitative research. Qualitative research—interviews, surveys, observations, etc.—sometimes gets a bad rap in quantitative policy schools like Harris, which breaks this trained social scientist's heart. One of the most important things I did with the teams I worked on at GAO was help them figure out when qualitative research would be helpful and when it wouldn't. Making a case for qualitative research got much tougher as narratives about the power of "big data" became more common. What I used to tell my teams, though, was that big data can't answer questions for which the data are fundamentally ill suited to answer. A simple way I found to frame this was to say that quantitative research is helpful in determining *what* is happening. Qualitative research, in turn, is helpful in understanding the underlying *why*. GAO often used quantitative and qualitative research in conjunction, which I thought made for stronger policy stories. Sometimes, though, qualitative research can do the job all by itself, so please don't discount it as "soft" or insufficiently rigorous. I lost track of how many times teams I designed surveys that captured the entire population being studied. It doesn't get more rigorous than that.

Another thing to keep in mind is that when identifying cause, you may look for the underlying reason why things are not working as expected, or you may need to find out why an intervention or program—or environmental, social, or economic conditions—caused something to happen or not happen and the extent to which the intervention, program, or condition causes the changes.

Policy analysts usually aren't satisfied with the first cause they come across—either because that cause is actually the *result* of the condition or because there is another cause that precedes it. Driven policy analysts will keep digging, keep asking why, and will eventually, if they're persistent, get closer to the *root* cause of a policy challenge. One way to look at this is to consider it from a diagnostic perspective, the way a medical doctor might. Can you imagine how unsatisfied you'd be if, when you became sick, all your doctor did was ask you why you thought you were sick? "Well, I ate a gas-station burrito yesterday for lunch," you might say. The doctor would then answer, "That must be it. The solution? No more burritos for you!" The burrito might have caused your sickness, but what if it didn't? This example may seem silly, but I've seen plenty of policy analysts fall victim to such thinking. Instead of grasping for the first plausible explanation, we need to run further tests and ask hard questions. Only after we've uncovered the root cause of a policy challenge can we then feel reasonably assured that our recommendation will help redress it.

A descriptive policy answer needs only a condition because a descriptive policy answer will not result in a policy recommendation. That doesn't mean, of course, that it isn't a valuable undertaking to provide readers with a descriptive policy answer. Helping the readers understand what is happening can be a hugely important contribution. Evaluative and prescriptive policy solutions, on the other hand, require you to include *all four* elements of a policy finding if you want to persuade your readers to implement your policy recommendation.

4. Effect: Answers the question "What will likely happen next?"

The effect question looks into the future: What will likely happen if the policy recommendation is or is not implemented? If you want readers to take your policy recommendations seriously, you must make sure the effect you discuss—either positive or negative—convincingly shows that action needs to be taken. Table 4.2 presents some language for doing this.

Which approach do you think is better: discussing the positive effects that could result from implementing your policy recommendation or laying out what negative effects could come from maintaining the status quo or implementing another policy recommendation? The short answer, I think, is that it depends. You'll need to use your judgment based on your audience and purpose. You can frame the effect positively for your readers: here's the benefit they can expect to receive (or a negative consequence they can expect to avoid). Or you can frame things negatively by telling readers that if they don't follow the recommendation, they can expect more poor outcomes (or miss out on some benefit). I've personally had more success with positive effect statements, mostly because I think my readers want to be inspired. They want to believe they have agency and can choose to make the future better than the past. Framing effects positively doesn't always work, of course. Sometimes readers need to comprehend that the consequences of inaction outweigh the risks of acting.

TABLE 4.2. Effective lead-in words and phrases to explain the effect and inspire action

Word or phrase	Example
Without...	Without an understanding of what is working, it will be difficult for agency leadership to develop a strategy for how to spend limited federal funds.
Unless...	Unless the US Department of Health and Human Services monitors states while they implement new foster care provisions, the department will not have sufficient information to determine how well these approaches are working and whether changes to state or federal policies—or federal guidance and assistance—are needed to improve outcomes for children in foster care.
In the absence of...	In the absence of sustained, ongoing revisions and adjustments in response to advances in medicine and changes in the labor market, the Department of Veterans Affairs' disability rating schedule risks continued waste and ineffectiveness.
If..., then...	If the Social Security Administration fails to evaluate the effectiveness of the changes it made to better detect and prevent misuse, then the administration risks wasting its scarce resources on activities that may be ineffective over the long term.

THE THIRD AND FINAL STEP IN HUMAN-CENTERED DESIGN: ANSWERING THE QUESTION

The last step is answering the question, which in our case is this one:

How could the United States plan to respond to future international food emergencies so that people facing food insecurity receive timely, cost-effective, and appropriate assistance?

To answer this question, we need to review the results of our affinity clustering and stakeholder mapping and focus on any evidence that shows us how to deliver food aid—whether it's in-kind or in the form of cash transfers and food vouchers—in a way that is timely, cost-effective, and appropriate. Let's imagine that a summary of your findings looks something like that presented in table 4.3.

TABLE 4.3. USAID food aid and the four elements of our policy story

Condition: *What's happening?*

Timeliness

- Distributing cash transfers or vouchers (or buying food locally) resulted in a time savings of nearly 14 weeks (a 62 percent gain), according to one study. The study also showed that buying grains locally saved over 50 percent, on average, whereas procuring processed commodities was not always cost-effective.

Cost-Effectiveness

- Cash transfers were least expensive, according to several rigorous studies that compared the relative costs of in-kind food aid, cash transfers, and food vouchers, though most of the studies did not account for the full costs associated with each modality.
- One study of a project in Niger found that food transfers were least expensive overall. Another study, of a project in Malawi, reported mixed results, finding that cash was more cost-effective but that food transfers were more cost-efficient. The third study, of a project in Bangladesh, did not identify the least expensive modality.
- A study of a food aid project in Yemen reported that recipients of cash transfers bought food items of greater variety and of higher nutritional value, which showed that cash transfers provided significantly greater improvements in dietary quality than did food transfers. The Yemen study also found that food transfers provided higher levels of caloric intake than did cash transfers, which the study's authors attributed to the relatively inexpensive staples, such as wheat and oil, included in the food transfers.
- A study of a food project in Niger found that food transfers resulted in significantly greater improvements in dietary quality than did cash transfers, which showed that food transfers provided a more varied and higher-quality diet. The researchers attributed this finding to the fact that cash recipients in Niger bought significantly cheaper bulk grains with their transfers than food recipients did. The study's authors determined that the cash beneficiaries purchased these cheap bulk grains in anticipation of seasonal price increases—stocking up on supplies for the "hungry" season. As a result, the food recipients, who relied on the food transfers provided by the project, had a more varied and higher-quality diet.

(continued)

TABLE 4.3. (*cont.*)

Appropriateness
- A study in Ecuador found that, compared with the control group, all recipients of cash transfers, food vouchers, and food transfers experienced significantly improved outcomes in terms of the value and volume of food consumed, caloric intake, and dietary diversity. Similarly, a study in Bangladesh found that all recipients of cash transfers, food transfers, or combinations of the two modalities experienced significantly improved outcomes for value and volume of food and for caloric intake.
- Among six studies that used control groups to examine the value and volume of food provided, five showed statistically significant improvements as a result of receiving all three types of assistance. Similarly, three of the six studies that used control groups to examine caloric intake also found statistically significant improvements for all three modalities.
- A study of a project in Niger comparing the effects of the three modalities found that food transfers provided the greatest dietary diversity, while studies of projects in Malawi, Uganda, and Yemen found that cash transfers provided greater dietary diversity than food transfers.

Criteria: *What should be happening?*
- American food aid should be timely, cost-effective, and appropriate to the specific conditions and limitations of the area where people are experiencing food insecurity.

Cause: *Why is the condition happening? What is causing the disparity between the condition and the criteria?*
- Contextual factors, such as the severity of the food crisis, the capacity of local markets, and changes in those markets, may have contributed to a variety of food security outcomes, showing that no food aid modality consistently outperformed the others.

Effect: *What will likely happen if the policy recommendation is or is not implemented?*
- Until research can provide a clear understanding of when different modalities of food aid should be used and why, based on rigorous data and analysis, we won't know whether the billions of dollars of aid the United States donates each year will have the desired effects of alleviating hunger and improving food security.

When the findings are taken all together, it seems to me that the story we'd want to tell is that there is no obvious strategy that will work in every country and in any situation. "The key is flexibility and choice," said Chris Barrett, a Cornell University economist who has studied US international food assistance. A core problem, he added, is the "one size fits all" approach that the US food aid system has taken historically whereby in-kind aid was the one and only answer to every food security problem. Instead, Barrett argued for years, humanitarian assistance organizations should be able to choose among food aid shipped from the United States, food purchased locally or regionally, and vouchers and cash transfers—depending on the situation and specific objectives. "While agricultural constituencies are reluctant to reform food aid," said Barrett, with the creation of the Emergency Food Security Program, "we're effectively moving it into the foreign assistance budget." Rather than take on farming and shipping lobbyists head on, it seems the United States has been "slowly making the transition, through a back door, from a farm-oriented food-aid policy to a development-oriented one," Barrett concluded. "And that's no bad thing."[16]

As you can tell from this case study, the policy analysts, advocates, and decision makers who led the effort to expand the use of cash transfers and food vouchers acted as "decentralizers," in the parlance of Aaron Wildavsky, author of *Speaking Truth to Power.* Given all the uncertainty and the lack of reliable data that could prove, definitively, which path would lead us to the right model of food aid, the analysts believed—or at least acted in accordance with the belief—that it was better to advocate for relatively small reforms, to tap into the knowledge of people in the field, to experiment, and to make adjustments based on the results of those experiments. And they did all that while also trying to ease the tension among objectives and resources, politics and planning, dogma and skepticism. To put it another way, they favored modest improvement over potential calamity. "Thinking that social ills are puzzles that can be solved," Wildavsky writes, "instead of problems that may be alleviated or eventually superseded, can make us despondent when they do not yield to our ministrations. A good comparison is to do something, as opposed to nothing, and then evaluate the result. The rub there is that you don't know whether some other action might have been better or worse. A better comparison is to contrast the problems we have now with those we had before."[17] We should consider proposed policy solutions, he concludes, "not as eternal truths but as hypotheses subject to modification and replacement by better ones until these in turn are discarded."[18]

CHAPTER 5

How to Haunt Your Readers

These are hard times we're living in. It's a hard time for facts. A hard time for meaningful, honest words, too. Both have been devalued and distorted. As someone who lives—and makes my living—by the integrity and authority of facts and words, it's this devaluation and distortion that feels most disorienting.

Some days it feels like the chaos happening all around us has so devalued what I do—and what you do—that it no longer matters whether I do it. When I see neighbors from my hometown, people I thought I knew, spreading conspiracy theories on Facebook or carrying weapons to the state capitol to shout fascist slogans at a governor who is trying, under tremendous pressure, to do the most good for the most people, I can't help but feel crushed under the fear of what might happen next week or next year. On my worst days, I feel guilty I brought three children into such a world.

The only thing that brings me to my writing desk each morning is the thought that facts *can* defend themselves against desecration, but only if we, as policy analysts and writers, can figure out how to communicate with those who may not share our experiences and worldviews. I believe we must all dedicate ourselves to the craft of good storytelling and to using meaningful words to fight against lies, obfuscation, misinformation, profane gibberish, and fear.

What makes for a good story, you might ask? Why do certain stories *stick* and others don't? I listened to an interview that author Ta-Nehisi Coates (of *Between the World and Me* fame) gave soon after George Floyd was murdered by police in Minneapolis. Something he said about the power of good stories deserves to be quoted in full:

I've always said that my objective as a writer is not merely to write in such a way that people read it and they say, "Yeah, I think that's correct." It's to write in such a way that people are haunted—that they go to bed thinking about it, that they wake up thinking about it, that they tell their spouses about it, that they tell their children about it, and their friends about it. And they grab them by the arm and say, "You *have* to read it."

To put his point another way: a good story haunts readers—that is, really *sticks* with them long after they finish reading—making them give a damn.

In this chapter I explain the dramatic arc, which is a way of structuring stories. Fashioning a dramatic arc lets me write stories that not only mix personal narrative with academic theory and observed facts based on rigorous data analysis but that also help the reader make better sense of the world. In the story reproduced below,[1] I analyzed the prevalence of white nationalists in the US military for The War Horse, an award-winning nonprofit newsroom educating the public on military service, war, and its impact. I'm proud of this story because its vividness gives it sticking power. Not long after it was published, a producer for the National Geographic Channel reached out to me for an interview for a new documentary on white nationalism and domestic terrorism in the United States. She told me she had read my story, and the thought of white nationalists trained to kill by the military had kept her up the night after she read it. She recalled a line from the story that had haunted her: " 'A drop of cyanide in your drink.' I couldn't stop thinking about that." The story begins thus:

> Prosecutors said the lieutenant was a self-proclaimed white nationalist. They said he was obsessed with neo-fascist and neo-Nazi views and that he spent untold hours online not only reading the manifesto of Anders Behring Breivik—a white supremacist who killed 77 people in Norway in 2011—but also meticulously researching how best to carry out a series of attacks against liberal politicians and hosts of cable news programs. They said he had been dreaming of a way, in his own words, "to kill almost every last person on earth." They claimed, and intended to prove, that had law enforcement not arrested him

when they did, he would have murdered innocent civilians "on a scale rarely seen in this country."[2]

In his defense, his lawyers said that despite having stockpiled a cache of weapons and ammunition, and even though he had called for "focused violence" to "establish a white homeland," he never would have actually attacked anyone. "This case," one of his lawyers said, "has been mischaracterized and sensationalized from the start." He was not a potential domestic terrorist, they said; instead, he was a "once-stellar and respected career military man unhinged in recent years by opioid abuse," which "poisoned his tolerance for racial and religious diversity and caused him to fantasize about atrocities he did not intend to commit."[3]

Prosecutors requested that the 50-year-old U.S. Coast Guard lieutenant, Christopher Hasson, receive 25 years in federal prison. "The eyes of many await this court's sentence," one of the prosecutors, Thomas Windom, noted. "The law-abiders await. The potential victims await. And white supremacists intending to perpetrate violent acts await to see exactly how much federal time they may be looking at in assessing whether and how to act on their violent beliefs."[4]

THE DRAMATIC ARC

Sometimes I'll start writing a story—or what I think might make a good story—only to run out of steam. Sometimes I stop because I lose interest in the subject or because I don't think what I have to say about it is all that important, even though I know in the back of my mind that probably isn't true. When this happens, I reach for one of the most tried-and-true formulas for writing a story that matters: the dramatic arc.

Jane Alison is a professor of creative writing at the University of Virginia, and in March 2019 she had an essay published in the *Paris Review* that briefly lays out the history of the dramatic arc. "Twenty-five hundred years ago," she writes, "Aristotle dissected tragedies such as Sophocles' *Oedipus the King* to find their common features, as he might dissect snakes to see if their spines were alike. He found that powerful dramas shared certain elements, including a particular path."[5] In the *Poetics*, Aristotle described what his dissections revealed: "A tragedy is an imitation of an action that is complete in itself [with a] beginning, middle, and end . . . Every tragedy is in part Complication and in part Dénouement; the incidents before the opening scene, and often certain also of those within the play, forming the Complication; and the rest the Dénouement. By Complication I mean all from the beginning of the story to the point just before the change in the hero's fortunes; by Dénouement, all from the beginning of the change to the end."[6] In dramatic stories a situation arises—either by cause or coincidence—tension builds and then reaches a peak, some action is taken, and then there is dénouement, a French word meaning "untying the knot."

The dramatic arc—with its inciting event, progressive complications, crisis, climax, and resolution—is not the only way to structure a story that has the power to haunt a reader. I have found in my classes and in my own writing, however, that if the goal is to tell policy stories that create connection and understanding and spur readers to take meaningful action, the five components of the dramatic arc—what I call the Five Essentials of Storytelling—are perfectly suited to the task. Unless writers use the Five Essentials, they risk presenting a story that may confuse, unsettle, or simply bore the reader.

The first essential of storytelling: The inciting event

The purpose of the inciting event is to upset the balance or routine of the protagonist. In the process, if told well, the inciting event will have a similar effect on readers. It will show readers there is something out there—something they might not have known about—that they'll need to make sense of by the end of the story. What do they think is true that absolutely isn't? What is something they do not understand? What is something that seems innocuous but is really a problem?

An inciting event can occur in two ways: either (1) it occurs as the result of a choice that you or another character makes or (2) it's a coincidence—that is, something unexpected, random, or accidental happens. Your goal should be to situate readers in a specific time and place so they can easily understand the landscape—both physical and emotional—as quickly as possible.

It's also important to note that if you want your readers to remember what happened in the inciting event, you must present them with specific and intimate details. Your readers must be able to take such details in and conjure images in their own minds. Any details you can present that evoke the essence of a memorable truth about the characters you're writing about or the situation they're in—those are the kind of details you want to include.

The second essential of storytelling: The progressive complications

In this section of the story, your readers are looking for context and background, but not too much. If they've made it through your inciting event, they're likely invested in the story and want to see how the action unfolds, but they probably won't stick around if the progressive complications drag on or if they seem irrelevant to the situation at hand. Your goal should be to ratchet up the tension. Sometimes you can accomplish this by presenting interesting background information that shows readers how you got to the inciting event. Other times it's best to move forward from the inciting event in chronological order. How much does your reader already know about your topic? If your topic is not particularly well known, it's probably better to include more background. If your topic has received lots of media coverage, it's probably better not to slow down your story with a history lesson.

My story for The War Horse continues:

> The U.S. military has a problem it doesn't want to acknowledge: Despite increased efforts to bar them from enlisting, white nationalists have continued to infiltrate all branches of the U.S. military. According to a recent poll conducted by Militarytimes.com, 36 percent of the 1,630 active-duty troops it surveyed reported they had personally witnessed examples of "white nationalism or ideological-driven racism within the ranks in recent months."[7] If this same percentage is extrapolated to the whole population of active-duty troops (about 1.3 million in December 2019), that would mean nearly half a million troops have witnessed examples of white nationalism in the ranks in recent months.
>
> A couple of months before Militarytimes.com published the results of its poll, a few West Point cadets and Naval Academy midshipmen were seen flashing what was viewed as a white power hand signal behind ESPN's Rece Davis, while he was broadcasting live before the

annual Army-Navy football game. Two days later, Defense Secretary Mark Esper was asked by a reporter whether he had heard anything about the incident and if he thought white supremacy in the military was an issue.

"I don't believe it's an issue in the military," he said.

When he was the Secretary of the Army, Esper continued, "We screened very closely and diligently the new recruits coming into the service," and in cases where someone with white-nationalist beliefs slipped through the cracks, the Uniform Code of Military Justice would be used to root them out.[8]

A search of incidents of white nationalism in the U.S. military since the terrorist attacks of Sept. 11, 2001, reveals dozens of cases of white nationalists in the military—and these are just the examples of troops who have been caught, written about in the media, and punished. If we are to believe that up to 36 percent of troops today have recently witnessed white nationalism or ideological-driven racism in the ranks, we must also conclude that the vast majority of white nationalists in the military not only slip through the cracks during the recruitment process, but that they also remain undetected, unaccounted for, and unpunished.

The truth is that no one knows how prevalent white nationalism is in the U.S. military. During a hearing of the House Armed Services Subcommittee on Military Personnel in February 2020, representatives of Naval Criminal Investigative Service and the Army's Criminal Investigation Division testified they had no reliable data on how many troops have been administratively discharged for promoting white supremacist ideologies. The Marine Corps, which has seen its fair share of white nationalism among its ranks, does not track the number of Marines it discharges for ties to white nationalist groups.

Troops who are caught with ties to white nationalism are typically punished by their commanders for violating Article 92 of the Uniform Code of Military Justice. This rule prohibits military personnel from promoting or participating in groups that advocate "illegal discrimination based on race, creed, color, sex, religion, ethnicity, or national origin" as well as groups that advocate "the use of force, violence, or criminal activity or otherwise advance efforts to deprive individuals of their civil rights."[9] Troops who violate this prohibition can be reprimanded, have their security clearances revoked, or be discharged from the military. Troops may also be punished under Article 134 for engaging in conduct that is discrediting and prejudicial to good order and discipline. The severity of the punishment a white nationalist receives—and whether they're punished at all—depends entirely on their commanders, who have almost complete discretion over how any violations are investigated, prosecuted, and adjudicated.

For the Department of Defense to know for certain how many troops are punished for their white nationalist activities, it would need to tally the number of troops punished under Articles 92 and 134, but even that number would only count those who were caught and punished. That number would also leave out all troops who were caught engaging in white nationalist activities but whose commanders did not feel the alleged behavior warranted further investigation or punishment.

Military officials always say the numbers of white nationalists in the ranks are small, "and because of that, it is not a priority," Carter F. Smith told *The New York Times* in 2019. Smith now teaches criminal justice at Middle Tennessee State University, but before that he served for 30 years as an Army criminal investigator. "Well, the numbers might be small," Carter continued, "but they are like a drop of cyanide in your drink. They can do a lot of damage."[10]

To help prevent such damage, the Obama administration allocated $10 million in 2016 to 31 different organizations that combat domestic extremism at the local level around the country. The next year, however, President Trump froze the funding while his administration reconsidered the grantees' applications. When the Trump administration released a revised list of organizations that would be receiving the funding, 12 of the 31 original organizations learned that their funding had been pulled. One of the organizations—Life After Hate—was one of the only original 31 that focuses on combating far-right extremism. Another organization that had its funding cut was the Chicago-based Hope Not Hate, which works to deradicalize neo-Nazis. The University of North Carolina at Chapel Hill also had funding cut that would have gone toward combating jihadist and white supremacist recruiting.

Under President Trump, the Department of Homeland Security's

Office of Community Partnerships also saw its budget slashed. During Obama's administration, the office led efforts to combat extremism in the United States with a budget of $21 million and a staff of 16 full-time employees and 25 contractors. The Trump administration slashed its budget to less than $3 million, cut the number of staff to eight full-time employees, and rebranded the office as The Office of Terrorism Prevention Partnerships. The office's former director, George Selim, resigned in June 2017. He told *NPR* that the environment in the office had become "too polarized," and he believed he could no longer do his job effectively.[11]

After the Christchurch mosque terrorist attacks in New Zealand in March 2019, President Trump was asked whether he believed white nationalism was a growing threat. "I don't, really," he said. "I think it's a small group of people that have very, very serious problems."[12]

For years, there's been a visceral response from politicians that if white nationalist groups are "being labeled as 'right wing,' then it's Republicans who are responsible for those groups' activities," Jason Blazakis told *Time*. Blazakis is the former director of the Counterterrorism Finance and Designations Office at the State Department, and is now a professor at the Middlebury Institute. "It's unfortunate," Blazakis continued, "but I think in many ways this has resulted and served this reluctance in the Republican side to take as strong of action as they could."[13]

The third and fourth essentials of storytelling: The crisis and climax

The crisis is the point in the story when a decision absolutely must be made. That decision will determine the course of the rest of the story, taking someone either closer or farther away from a positive outcome. It's the moment of truth—the moment readers have been waiting for. More than anything, they want to see how the costs and benefits are weighed and what is ultimately decided. You'll know when you've found a genuine crisis when it's possible for something bad to happen regardless of what decision is made.

The climax, in turn, is the point in the story where the decision is made, where the question raised by the crisis is answered. The climax should also contain the immediate result of the decision. What happened

next? Keep in mind that it's not such a good idea to allude to the decision made and the immediate outcome. Your readers will want to see
for themselves what happened.

> The Department of Defense has taken some positive steps to keep
> white nationalists out of the military. Recruiters are required to
> check the criminal records of all recruits, though only recruits who
> had been charged with a crime related to white nationalism would be
> found out. All military recruits are also subjected to a psychological
> examination that could uncover aberrant or extremist beliefs and are
> required to fill out a lengthy questionnaire—called an SF-86—that
> asks them: "Are you now or have you EVER been a member of an
> organization dedicated to terrorism, either with an awareness of the
> organization's dedication to that end, or with the specific intent to
> further such activities?"
>
> It's unclear, however, how this self-reported information is
> corroborated, if at all. Moreover, according to Heidi L. Beirich of the
> non-profit Global Project Against Hate and Extremism, "members
> of white supremacist groups may not view their activity as related to
> terrorism," which could undermine the intent of the questions in the
> first place.[14]
>
> Military recruiters are also trained to be on the lookout for tattoos
> associated with white nationalism, including lightning bolts, skulls,
> and swastikas, though there is no tattoo database for them to consult.
>
> Perhaps the biggest blind spot the military has when evaluat-
> ing the ideological fitness of a recruit or current soldier pertains to
> social media use. Instead of using rallies, white-power concerts, and
> militarized compounds, the current generation of white nationalists
> needs only their smartphones, an anonymous screenname, a forum
> like 8chan or 4chan, and an endless appetite for offensive behavior to
> recruit and mobilize its members.

The fifth essential of storytelling: The resolution

We all need resolution, and so do stories. "A life without temporal
boundaries," explains philosopher Samuel Scheffler, "would be no more
a life than a circle without a circumference would be a circle."[15] The

resolution is the part of the story where we attempt to make sense of all that has happened in the story. If the inciting event shows the reader the *before*, the resolution is where the reader gets to see the *after*—or at least what the after could look like. A resolution, in turn, could come in the form of a memorable anecdote that clarifies the key point of the story. It could also come from a telling detail that symbolizes something larger than itself or suggests how the story might move forward in the future. The resolution might echo the beginning to give readers a sense that the story has come full circle. Readers love that symmetry. Just remember that readers want to learn how the problem that incited the dramatic arc got resolved. Once they know, they'll probably stop reading—so stop writing once you've provided a resolution.

After three white soldiers stationed at Fort Bragg in North Carolina were convicted of committing two racially motivated murders in December 1995, the Department of Defense created a task force to investigate neo-Nazis in the military. What they found were persisting "indications of extremist and racist attitudes among soldiers."[16] In response, the department gave commanders more discretion to report suspected extremist beliefs or racist behaviors among their troops. In 2000, the Department of the Army released updated guidance on a range of issues related to extremism, including information on tattoos that were no longer acceptable and how commanders should handle instances of their troops engaging in extremist activity.

But before any steps to quell the spread of white nationalism in the military can be taken, the Department of Defense first needs to measure the problem. Until the military knows approximately how many white nationalists it has in its ranks, the threat will continue to have a destructive effect not only on the morale, unit cohesion, and combat readiness of the military, but also on relations between troops and the rest of the country.

"Today's white supremacists in the military," one Department of Defense investigator told the Southern Poverty Law Center, "become tomorrow's domestic terrorists once they're out."[17]

CHAPTER 6

How to Structure Policy Memos and Briefs for Maximum Impact

When I was still working at the Government Accountability Office, a colleague of mine had an interesting way of explaining to the analysts she worked with how a policy report should be structured. It all came done to anatomy and physiology. Anatomy, of course, is the study of living things and their parts. Physiology, on the other hand, is the more complicated study of how those parts function complementary to one another. When it comes to policy writing that matters, you must know both the anatomy (the parts) and the physiology (how the parts work together).

THE ANATOMY AND PHYSIOLOGY OF POLICY STORIES THAT MATTER

Title

The title should tell readers what action you propose they take. For example: "Veteran Suicide: The Department of Veterans Affairs Needs to Have Its Programs Independently Evaluated." If you're not making a policy recommendation, make sure your title reflects your most important key finding.

Executive summary

The most effective executive summaries begin with your policy recommendations or key findings. Simple as that. Simple, yes, but is it easy to do? Not necessarily. Let's look at a few examples of less-than-effective executive summaries:

> Until recently, relatively little was known about labor characteristics of wage-earning adults enrolled in Medicaid—a joint federal-state program that finances health care for low-income individuals—and wage-earning adults in households receiving food assistance from the federal Supplemental Nutrition Assistance Program (SNAP). According to Census Bureau data, the 12 million wage-earning Medicaid enrollees and the 9 million wage-earning SNAP recipients share a range of common labor characteristics. For example, approximately 70 percent of adult wage earners in both programs worked full-time hours on a weekly basis and about one-half of them worked full-time hours annually. In addition, 90 percent of wage-earning adults participating in one of these programs was employed in the private sector (compared to 81 percent of nonparticipants) and 72 percent worked in one of five main industries, according to an analysis of program participation data included in the Census Bureau's 2019 Current Population Survey. Across 11 states, the percentage of working adult Medicaid enrollees and SNAP recipients working for any one employer did not exceed 4 percent in any state that provided data, according to a non-generalizable analysis of program data from February 2020.

I see this kind of thing a lot. Instead of starting with the recommendation or key findings, the writer focuses more on where the data came from and what the data tell us. There's not much in the way of context or explanation. What does it all mean? It's hard to say. The findings *could* be compelling, but it's not clear how or why. Perhaps these findings could be used to complicate a stereotypical narrative that many believe about social welfare recipients. Or perhaps these findings indicate some larger problem with economic mobility or income inequality. Until the writer tells us what it all means, we're not likely to care about the analysis behind the data.

> Global temperature has increased over the past 60 years, and this observed increase is due primarily to human-induced emissions of heat-trapping gases. With increases in global temperature come changes

to the climate around the world. In the United States, changes to the climate are already affecting water, energy, transportation, agriculture, ecosystems, and health, among other sectors. Climate change in these various sectors will likely combine with pollution, population growth, overuse of resources, urbanization, and other social, economic, and environmental stresses to create impacts larger than can be accurately predicted. The amount and rate of future climate change depend on current and future human-caused emissions of heat-trapping gases and airborne particles.

This writer, to the detriment of the executive summary, provides readers with a list of facts stacked one on top of the other—all without context or clear links. The writer has left it to the readers to tie it all together and decide what the policy story is trying to say. Something I tell my students again and again is *data can't speak for themselves.*

Crime and society's response to it pose significant costs to the United States. In fiscal year 2012, the Department of Justice's Bureau of Justice Statistics reported that federal, state, and local governments collectively spent over $280 billion (adjusted to 2016 dollars) on criminal justice programs, including police protection, the court system, and incarceration. There are also many other financial and nonfinancial effects of crime in the United States that researchers consider when estimating the total costs of crime, including tangible costs like replacing damaged property or medical care to treat victims' injuries. There are also intangible costs, such as changes in people's behavior to avoid crime, among many other costs. Based on a literature review and a survey of experts, we found there is no commonly used approach for estimating the costs of crime. There are also multiple challenges that complicate efforts to estimate costs, according to the experts surveyed. As a result, researchers have estimated varying annual costs of crime, including totals of $690 billion, $1.57 trillion, and $3.41 trillion, adjusted to 2016 dollars.

This is by far the most common mistake I see policy writers make in their executive summaries. This writer has used what is sometimes called the *funnel technique,* where they begin with a broad claim or background information or some historical facts and then narrow their way to the point they are making in the document. The problem with that is you cannot know for sure whether your readers—especially if they are skeptical or short on time—are going to have the patience to work through the preliminary material to arrive at your recommendations or key findings. That's a risk I'm not willing to take in my own writing.

After you've made it clear to readers, right up front, what policy intervention is necessary to implement, the next thing you need to do is tell them that something new has happened or something has changed. This signals to readers that there's a problem—an *instability*. Have there been changes in laws or in regulations, the effects of which are unknown? Has there been a controversy about which we need more information if there is to be any resolution? What don't we know? Why might we need to know it? In short, why should the reader care?

What your policy report should promise is stability—a viable solution to the problem that will have positive effects for the reader.

Background and methodology

The background and methodology section of a policy report serves two functions. First, it offers the reader additional context—just enough information about the subject at hand. Focus on helping the reader understand (1) what regulatory and legislative landscape is relevant to the focus of the report; (2) who the key players are, what role they play, and how they're related to one another; and (3) how we got to where we are today. Second, it offers readers details about the methodology you used to collect and analyze the data that underpins your findings. Did you conduct a survey? Is it representative? Did you run a regression analysis? Walk readers through that. Did you interview anyone? How did you select interviewees?

You can shorten almost any policy report by keeping the background and methodology section as short as possible. In some cases, especially in policy memos or one-pagers, you may choose to omit this section. If your reader is familiar with the background already, and if you did not use any sophisticated data collection and analysis tools, you should transition from the executive summary straight into the key findings.

Key findings

In the key findings section, each paragraph needs to be written deductively (more on that in chapter 7), which means that the main point of the paragraph is presented in the first sentence. The remaining sentences in the paragraph present the data, facts, and statistics, as well as your analysis and reasoning (and any context needed), that prove the point you made in the first sentence.

In the example below, imagine that your client is a nongovernmental organization tasked with administering food aid efficiently and effectively in parts of the world ravaged by natural disasters or civil wars. The client wants to know whether it's best to provide food or cash to those affected. Note that the criteria are not explicitly stated because "what should be happening" is implied (i.e., people affected by natural disasters and civil wars should be efficiently and effectively served by your client). This paragraph presents evidence suggesting that the best strategy is to combine the two methods of food aid delivery:

Condition	**When food aid needs to be administered in countries where inflation is rampant, providing it in the form of cash and food has been shown to be more effective than providing cash alone.**
Evidence and analysis	In January 2010, Rachel Sabates-Wheeler and Stephen Devereux published the results of a study they conducted on Ethiopia's Productive Safety Net Programme. Their team of researchers conducted a regression analysis on a two-wave panel survey conducted in 2006 and 2008. The data show specifically that food transfers enabled higher levels of income growth, livestock accumulation, and self-reported food security. **This may be partially explained by the fact that the cash transfers that were studied**
Cause	**were not indexed, meaning they did not adjust to inflation.** A reliance on cash transfers that are not indexed to deliver social protection in an infla-
More evidence	tionary environment "is not an optimal strategy," the researchers noted, "because commodity-based transfers retain their value whereas the purchasing

Effect

power of cash transfers is eroded by rising commodity pricing" (Sabates-Wheeler & Devereux, 2010). **Until nongovernmental organizations are afforded the flexibility to provide food aid in the combined form of cash and food, they may miss out on opportunities to deliver food aid as efficiently and effectively as possible.**

Both at the Government Accountability Office and at the Harris School, I've found that policy writers can get overwhelmed and confused about what to include in the key findings and what not to. I'm sorry to say that I can't give you a formula to follow here. What I can give you is a bit of advice. The most relevant information to include in a key findings section is information that offers the reader

- evidence, data, and analysis to support your conclusion;
- background, context, and reasoning that make sense of the evidence; and
- consideration—and rebuttal—of divergent points of view.

You'll know that you have *enough* information in your key findings section when you have answered the questions you set out to answer with just enough supporting evidence. Sounds simple, but it takes practice.

Here's another example having to do with Medicare expenditures. Notice how this key findings section presents the main point first, offers evidence to support the main point, and then presents a cause (based on a regression analysis) and a likely effect:

Condition

From 2007 through 2013, Medicare expenditures for services offered by hospital outpatient departments (HOPDs) grew rapidly, increasing from $22.4 billion to $36.3 billion, or about 8.3 percent annually. In comparison, over the same time period the American economy grew by an average annual rate of 2.4 percent, and total Medicare Part B spending grew by an average annual rate of 5.8 percent. This growth in Medicare expenditures for services offered by HOPDs can be

Cause   attributed to a general shift away from physicians providing services in their private offices to providing them through HOPDs. **Given that Medicare often pays providers at a higher rate—sometimes twice as much—when the same service is performed in an HOPD, hospitals are incentivized to acquire**

Context **private physician practices and/or hire physi-**
and   **cians as salaried employees—financial arrange-**
analysis **ments health care experts commonly refer to as vertical consolidation. Other factors, such as new payment policies that reward coordination, may also incentivize vertical consolidation.** If such practices continue, Medicare's long-term ability

Effect   to efficiently purchase health care for elderly Americans may be compromised.

The most important thing to remember about presenting your analysis and the evidence that underpins it is this: The reader *must* be able to see clearly the connection between your analysis and evidence and the main point you state in the first sentence. Whether your evidence is data you analyzed, mathematical proofs, another analyst's theories, or someone's exact words, the reader usually needs a little help to understand exactly how the evidence proves what you are saying is correct. Consider the difference between these two sentences:

Sentence 1: Some state legislatures have considered bills targeting pharmaceutical price gouging.

Sentence 2: The simplicity of the idea known as the extraterritoriality principle—that states only hold authority within their borders—belies the difficulty of the idea's application, and courts have struggled to define the extraterritoriality principle's precise scope.

Note that, in Sentence 1, the evidence you would need to prove the key finding would likely repeat the language of the key finding itself. "For example," you might write, "the Wisconsin state legislature considered bills targeting pharmaceutical price gouging in 2014, 2015, and 2019." See the unnecessary repetition? That's a result of the fact that

Sentence 1 does not make a doubtable claim. The evidence is literally evident in the claim. Contrast that with Sentence 2, which presents a key finding that will need more analysis to clarify *why* "courts have struggled" in applying this "idea." That's a good thing, by the way. It means that the key finding is nuanced enough to require explanation. If your policy report was full of sentences like Sentence 1, that would signal to me that your key findings aren't all that interesting—mostly because they're self-evident.

Sometimes writers run into problems when they prioritize their evidence over their key findings. This too you should avoid doing. Consider the next example, which illustrates what happens when a writer focuses more on the evidence than on what the evidence means. This writer was trying to argue that setting higher salaries for politicians will lead to better management of public funds. Unfortunately, that point gets lost in the explanation of the evidence:

> *Draft*: Gagliarducci and Nannicini, in their 2013 study, show that higher wages attract more educated candidates. They studied mayors of all Italian municipalities from 1993 to 2001 and found that a 33% increase in wage rate translated into 0.9 to 1.6 more years of education among candidates. It can be argued that laying restrictions on salaries will be a more economical use of public money. However, this can be deemed as a short-sighted approach. If such expenditures lead to increased efficiency and better performance, then in the long run increased salaries will prove to be a good investment. Better paid politicians down-size government machinery by improving internal efficiency. The above study was able to find evidence which showed that better compensated public officials were able to upgrade internal processes and improve efficiency of daily operations. In particular, the study found that such public officials were able to lower taxes and tariffs per capita (by about 13% and 86%, respectively) and reduce the amount of personnel and other current expenditures (by about 11% and 22%, respectively).

By introducing the evidence (i.e., Gagliarducci and Nannicini's 2013 study) in the first sentence, the writer places the key finding about higher-paid politicians in a secondary place. This arrangement leads the writer to bring information into the argument that doesn't help it: namely, the writer includes the data point of "more educated candidates"; unfortunately, "politician education" doesn't factor into the writer's primary argument about government efficiency and higher-paid politicians. Although the education factor may explain some of the researchers' findings, that explanation adds cognitive moves for the reader to make and thus clouds the writer's intended argument. Now consider the comparative expediency and logical simplicity that the revision below achieves by subordinating the grounds (or evidence) to the claim:

Revision: While common sense might suggest that increased politician salaries are not an economical use of public funds, a prominent study of Italian municipalities proves the opposite (Gagliarducci and Nannicini, 2013). Higher politician pay was strongly correlated with increased government efficiency and decreased superfluous bureaucratic expense: in particular, better compensated public officials lowered taxes and tariffs per capita (13% and 86%, respectively) and tended to reduce extraneous government expenditures by a total of 33 percent.

Another thing I see public policy writers do all the time is begin their key findings section with a discussion of their research methodology. As much as it pains me to tell someone who worked hard developing a randomized controlled trial and analyzing the resulting data that their research method is not driving the story, it is the truth. Your readers will only care about your methodology after they've learned what you found by using it.

The secret to focusing your key findings on the *actual* key findings is to devote the main clause of most sentences to the key actors and the actions they took (more on this in chapter 9). You can then supply ancillary information in subordinate clauses and phrases. Take this draft sentence, for example:

Draft: The April 2012 Executive Order required Veterans Affairs and other agencies to prevent abusive and deceptive recruiting practices that target the recipients of federal military and veteran education benefits by strengthening their enforcement and compliance efforts.

In the revised sentence, the main clause (italicized for emphasis) focuses on the actor and the action:

> *Revision: In 2014, Veterans Affairs launched a new system* that allows veterans to file complaints of abusive and misleading school recruiting practices and other violations of the Principles of Excellence, as required by an April 2012 Executive Order.

Above all else, try not to get ahead of the story. Don't write, for example, about the likely impact of your findings and so venture prematurely into your recommendations or conclusion. Devote all the precious space you have to your key findings alone.

Characterizing the condition is one of the toughest jobs you'll have as a policy analyst. You must be able to synthesize the information in such a way that readers will want to know about it. Doing so often requires discerning vocabulary choices, and it requires an appreciation for the context of the report. Is the program *fragmented*? Or just *differentiated*? Do programs work at *cross purposes*? Are you finding a lack of *coordination*? Or are you finding a lack of *collaboration*? Coordination and collaboration are not the same thing. Policy analysts are trained to find gaps between what is happening and what should be happening, but what is the nature of the gaps we find? Is there a *displacement*? Or is there a *misalignment* of purpose and function?

The Government Accountability Office characterizes the condition exceedingly well. In the example in the box (*opposite*), I'd like you to notice how incredibly effective—and efficient—the writer's use of evidence is in supporting the key finding. Why is the evidence effective? The evidence cited in box note 1 speaks directly to the key finding (namely, that accounting for inflation matters), which is to say the evidence is explicitly relevant. Box note 2 then follows this point by citing evidence from a source that the target readers will know: the Federal Accounting Standards Advisory Board. Once the readers, a federal department, see this source cited, they will need no further explanation for why they should accept the Government Accountability Office's argument to account for inflation.

Don't shortchange the work of arranging your key findings and their supporting evidence. The gift we can offer readers is shedding light on what is otherwise murky. That's the point of public policy writing that matters—to lift the veil of obscurity on a subject and to tell stories that help solve problems.

GAO report on the costs of income-driven repayment (IDR) student loan plans

Background

In light of a three-year, 10% increase in the number of student borrowers paying their federal loans by IDR plans, the Government Accountability Office (GAO) was tasked with reviewing the Department of Education's IDR budget estimates. Ultimately, GAO found a number of crucial budgeting factors Education had not taken into consideration when preparing their IDR budget—namely, a failure to "adjust income forecasts for inflation." These factors could cause a significant funding shortfall given the relative cost and growing popularity of IDR plans. As a result, the GAO report was structured around the primary claim / recommendation that Education needs to expand their budget estimates for IDR plans.

Key Finding

When asked, Education officials said they did not adjust income forecasts for inflation because they did not identify patterns in the estimated historical income data suggesting that incomes would be affected by inflation. Whether or not these patterns were evident when reviewing the data, there was inflation over the almost 20-year period covered by the historical dataset and there is likely to be inflation in the future.[1] Federal guidance for estimating subsidy costs stresses the importance of taking economic effects into account when estimating loan performance.[2] For IDR plan costs, this would include the extent to which inflation affects borrower incomes and payment amounts.

---

1. Education officials also said they did not incorporate inflation into their income forecasts because they believed that inflation would affect federal poverty guidelines and incomes similarly, mitigating inflation's effect on cost estimates. However, officials did not test this assumption. When we tested the impact of inflation on both borrower incomes and federal poverty guidelines, expected costs changed substantially.
2. Federal Accounting Standards Advisory Board, Credit Reform Task Force, Issue Paper: *Model Credit Program Methods and Documentation for Estimating Subsidy Rates and the Model Information Store*, 96-CR-7 (Washington, D.C.: May 1, 1996).

Headings for your key findings

To make it easier for your reader to skim your report, I suggest using headings for each section. For the executive summary, background and methodology, recommendations, and conclusion, you can use what I call *topical headings,* that is, headings that don't contain a verb. For the key findings, use headings that contain both a subject and a verb that describe what you found—not your methodology or the resulting recommendation. I call these *message-driven headings.* I've found that it's better to save recommendations for the recommendations section (and for the opening of the executive summary, of course). Headings should be as long as they *need* to be but as short as they *can* be. The way to be concise is to focus solely on the message, not the details. Save the explanations, qualifiers, specific data points, and other elements of the policy story for the body of the text. For example:

- The American Rescue Plan Act Will Help Millions and Bolster the Economy
- Medicaid Expansion Improves Postpartum Health Care Coverage and Access to Care
- The Proposed Housing Rule Would Result in Thousands of Children Losing Their Homes

Recommendations

Effective policy recommendations (1) identify feasible actions the readers should take and (2) provide the appropriate level of detail to facilitate implementation and subsequent follow-up. Other characteristics include those summarized in table 6.1.

Here's a formula I've used to draft recommendations:

To [*achieve your readers' goal*], the [*decision maker*] should [*your recommended action*], which will [*achieve the readers' goal or result in a desirable effect*].

TABLE 6.1. Characteristics of policy recommendations that matter

	Readers	Address your recommendation to a person or program so that it's clear who's responsible for acting on the recommendation.

	Purpose	Your recommendations must do three things:
		1. Address the root cause of the policy issue or challenge you identified.
		2. Connect clearly to the evidence.
		3. Be feasible, cost-effective, and measurable.

	Explanatory statement	Focus on concisely presenting *who* should do *what* and *why*. Avoid phrasing that reintroduces the barriers or challenges you identified. That information should be presented in the key findings section.

	Lead-in sentence	If you're making multiple recommendations, have a lead-in sentence that indicates their number, such as "We are making four recommendations to improve program operations: First, . . ."
		Consider arranging your recommendations in a numbered or bulleted list below the lead-in sentence.

	Clarity and precision	Choose apt phrasing (e.g., *explore* vs. *ensure* and *plan* vs. *implement* require different actions).
		Avoid being unnecessarily prescriptive. If you want to recommend that certain steps be taken, state that explicitly.
		If you want to recommend that the readers determine the course of action to meet your recommendation's intent, introduce possible steps with a phrase that makes it clear you are providing an example: *such as, for instance, for one,* etc.

Let's now consider how we might revise turgid, difficult-to-understand recommendations into ones that are clearer, more concise, and more persuasive. Note the coded emphases added to the revisions: **bold = the actor**; <u>underlined = what action to take</u>; and *italic = why the actor should take that action.*

Draft: Defining specific roles and responsibilities for both the hospital and the organization is crucial, as is selecting specific goals for the partnership. This was clear from our interviews and academic research (Torres and Margolin, 2003). The National Network of Hospital-based Violence Intervention Programs (NNHVIP) suggests selecting goals that follow the "SMART" criteria: specific, measurable, achievable, relevant, and time-framed (Karraker et al, 2011). Selecting clear objectives will help the University of Chicago Hospital's Trauma Center define effective relationships with partner organizations.

Revision: **The University of Chicago Hospital's Trauma Center** <u>should consult with its partner organizations</u> *to clearly define roles and responsibilities and establish goals for the partnership.* These goals should be based on SMART Criteria to ensure they are specific, measurable, achievable, relevant, and time-framed.

Draft: Given the size and relevance of the resources spent on aid to reduce conflict and the conclusions we drew from our study, we recommend the commission of a rigorous, large-scale randomized controlled trial, which currently does not exist. This would cost only a small share of the resources currently spent on aid, but it would provide the most reliable type of evidence available on whether aid is effective for reducing conflict, and what types of aid seem to work best in which contexts. Such a study would facilitate an evidence-based decision-making process in the future and avoid investing resources in cost-ineffective projects.

Revision: **The Office of Foreign Assistance Resources** <u>should consider conducting a rigorous, large-scale randomized controlled trial</u> *to reliably and cost-effectively determine whether aid reduces conflict and what types of aid work best.*

———

Draft: We recommend making information on the region's transit system more accessible to users. This could include designing phone applications that allow paratransit users with smartphones to plan and book trips across different transportation modes and establishing call centers to enable paratransit users without smartphones to book their trips.

Other options include establishing call centers that allow users without smartphones to book rides via telephone and better integration of fixed route and rideshare services through applications that allow users to plan trips across modes.

Revision: **The Metropolitan Planning Council** <u>should make transit information more accessible to paratransit users</u> by, for example, (1) designing phone applications that integrate fixed route and rideshare services *so that users can better plan and book trips across different modes of transportation* and (2) establishing call centers for the same purpose that can be used by paratransit users who do not use smartphones.

Conclusion

To be most effective, conclusions should make it clear to your readers why it is important for them to act on your policy recommendations *now*. The conclusion is the last thing they will read before putting down your policy report. What is the lasting message you want them to take away from all the hard work you put into it?

One question I get from students all the time has to do with uncertainty. How can policy analysts possibly be certain that their recommendations and conclusions will make any difference when there is so much uncertainty in the world? Whenever someone asks me about this, I say the same thing: Everything we *think* we know about public policy is tentative. Absolutely *nothing* is carved in stone. We need to recognize this—and relish it, too. The reason we want to display confidence in our findings, recommendations, and conclusions is that uncertainty does not inspire confidence. We'd persuade no one of anything if every conclusion we wrote sounded like this: Although we have plenty of evidence to support this conclusion, and we feel highly confident that this evidence is reliable, it is possible—though we would argue highly improbable—that future studies and new evidence may compel us to revise our policy recommendation.

We'll never know with a hundred percent confidence whether our findings, conclusions, and recommendations will help and whether any will have unintended consequences that cost more than they benefit the people we're trying to help. One thing I do know for certain though is that refraining from making any recommendations at all, solely because you *might* be wrong, is never a good idea. Quibblers and naysayers don't make things happen. If you want your public policy writing to matter, you must take calculated risks. Table 6.2 summarizes the characteristics of effective conclusions.

TABLE 6.2. Characteristics of conclusions that matter

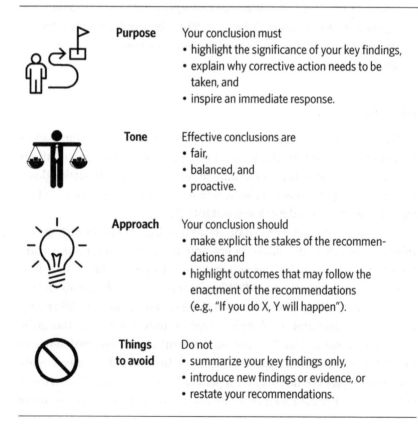

	Purpose	Your conclusion must • highlight the significance of your key findings, • explain why corrective action needs to be taken, and • inspire an immediate response.
	Tone	Effective conclusions are • fair, • balanced, and • proactive.
	Approach	Your conclusion should • make explicit the stakes of the recommendations and • highlight outcomes that may follow the enactment of the recommendations (e.g., "If you do X, Y will happen").
	Things to avoid	Do not • summarize your key findings only, • introduce new findings or evidence, or • restate your recommendations.

Another valuable thing you can do in the conclusion is offer a wider perspective on the topic at hand. What is the significance of your key findings taken as a whole? If you find it helpful, pretend you're a newspaper editor writing an editorial. Make your points as strongly as you can. The conclusion is not a place to mince words.

PUTTING IT ALL TOGETHER

Once you've got all your document's parts written, and now that you know how the parts work together, you have what you need to put your policy memo or brief together. The box below provides a handy template for starting its assembly.

Putting it all together: A policy memo template

A Title That Clearly States Your Key Finding or Policy Recommendation

Executive Summary

In the executive summary, state your recommendation; always start with your main point first. Then briefly summarize your main findings as answers to your readers' questions. Essentially, you are explaining why you are recommending they take action. End the summary with a brief statement of what will happen if the readers implement your recommendation.

Background and Methodology

Here you provide context and any historical or technical information the reader may need to understand your findings—and nothing more. Consider what your reader already knows. You may also need to explain where your data came from and how you analyzed them. Note that, depending on your findings, you may not need a background and methodology section.

Your Key Findings' Headings Should Be Complete Sentences with a Subject and a Verb

In the key findings section, answer your readers' questions directly. Also provide evidence (and the context for the evidence) and your analysis of the evidence in support of your descriptive, evaluative, or prescriptive answer. You may also need to admit any limitations to your findings and rebut alternative options if necessary.

(continued)

Putting it all together: A policy memo template (*cont.*)

Recommendations

Your recommendations should link the root causes of the readers' problem, which you identified in your key findings section, to *what* needs to be done by *whom*. Your recommendations should be feasible, cost-effective, and specific but not too narrow.

Conclusion

Your conclusion should place your key findings in a broader context that reminds the reader of the issue's importance. Why is it important that action be taken immediately? A good conclusion weighs loss aversion against hope for the future as motivating factors.

CHAPTER 7

Deductive and Unified Paragraphs

Public policy writing that matters is structured deductively so that readers can find the main point of every paragraph in the paragraph's first sentence. Structuring your paragraphs deductively will not only give your readers the content they need most right up front, but it will also help them make sense of the data, evidence, and analysis you must present to support the main point of the paragraph. Look at the paragraph below: Which sentence contains the main point?

> There is no central registry of military veterans, and the Department of Veterans Affairs (VA) cannot count all veterans because only about 50 percent register with the department after leaving the military. And while the U.S. Centers for Disease Control and Prevention and the Department of Defense have partnered with the VA to share databases to more accurately estimate the number of veterans who die by suicide, it's still an imperfect system. The best estimate we have is that 22 veterans die by suicide daily, and some data suggest the rate may be higher for veterans under the age of 30. The VA cannot accurately estimate the number of veterans who die by suicide without better data.

The main point comes at the end of the paragraph: "The VA cannot accurately estimate the number of veterans who die by suicide without better data." The author of this paragraph used an *inductive* structure, meaning they presented the main point last, after having traced the path they took in thinking through the finding.

We sometimes write this way because it can feel natural to record our thinking process, to lay out the proof for our argument. We talk this way all the time. When we tell stories or jokes or when we want to surprise someone with something unexpected, we start with the background information and lay out a path for the listener to follow. We don't start with the moral of the story or the punch line of the joke. There's a transaction taking place when we tell stories and jokes. Your listener expects to be entertained. In public policy writing, there is no such expectation. That doesn't mean, of course, that we should strive to bore readers. Instead, we should give them what they want right away, and what they want is the main point. They will stick around to hear what you have to say only after they understand your main point.

Take another look at the example paragraph above on the Department of Veterans Affairs' need for better data. Did you feel a little lost after a sentence or two? It's all right if you did. If you read it again, you'll notice that it's front-loaded with a series of facts and pieces of evidence—(1) there is no central registry, (2) only 50 percent of veterans register with the VA, and (3) the best estimate is that 22 veterans die by suicide daily. Without a deductive statement at the beginning to put everything into context, readers are left wondering what it all means and why they need to know it.

Conversely, when we write deductively (see the revised paragraph below), our readers can see why all the data, evidence, and analysis we present is important. Put another way, only after a reader knows what *we* think the data, evidence, and analysis mean (sentence in **boldface**) will they want to wade through that information to decide for themselves if the conclusion we reached was logical and persuasive.

> **The Department of Veterans Affairs (VA) cannot accurately estimate the number of military veterans who die by suicide without better data.** First, there is no central registry of veterans, and the VA cannot count all veterans because only about 50 percent register with the department after they leave the military. And while the U.S. Centers for Disease Control and Prevention and the Department of Defense have partnered with the VA to share databases to more accurately estimate the number of veterans who die by suicide, it is still an imperfect system. The best estimate we have is that 22

veterans die by suicide daily, and some data suggest the rate may be higher for veterans under the age of 30.

Writing with a consistently deductive structure will also help you write more unified paragraphs. What do I mean by unified? It's simple. A unified paragraph has one main point—and only one main point. Do yourself a favor and commit this mantra to memory: "One paragraph, one point." If you try to pack too much into a paragraph, your readers will feel like they're lost at sea, and readers don't like to feel that way.

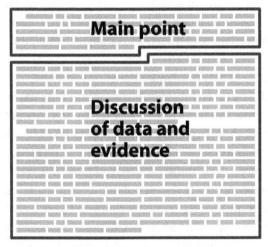

An illustration of deductive paragraph structure

TOPIC SENTENCES

The best way I know how to ensure that paragraphs are both deductive and unified is to write strong topic sentences. By beginning with a strong topic sentence, you'll be able to determine what you should include in the paragraph and, perhaps more importantly, what you should leave out.

It can be helpful to think about your reader's expectations and whether your paragraph fulfills them. If, after reading your topic sentence, your reader finds key terms and concepts developed in the remainder of the paragraph, then your writing will seem unified and logical. If, however, your reader does not find key terms and concepts developed in the subsequent sentences—or if they find other, unrelated key terms and concepts developed—your writing will seem disorganized and illogical.

One thing to keep in mind is that not all topic sentences are created equal. Some are so broad that the writer could write practically anything in the rest of the paragraph:

> *Draft*: Military veterans face many challenges when they return home from war.

> *Revision*: Some of the most pressing challenges veterans face when they return home include finding meaningful employment, reestablishing connections with friends and family, and alcohol abuse.

Sometimes you may need more than one sentence to introduce your main point. If you're writing about something complex, don't be afraid to take two sentences to introduce key terms and concepts. One thing to keep in mind, though: your readers likely will not base their expectations on the beginning of your first topic sentence. Therefore, if you are going to use more than one sentence, you must put your most important terms and concepts at the end of the second sentence.

One other thing to keep in mind is that you do not have to make your point more than once in a paragraph. Many of us were taught to add a concluding sentence to each paragraph that reiterates the main point. This is not necessary in public policy writing. Simply state your point, provide your data and evidence, and move on to the next paragraph.

CHAPTER 8

Coherent Paragraphs

Once you've mastered the art of writing deductively and limiting yourself to making one point per paragraph, you have accomplished a great deal. If, however, the sentences you write do not flow together, your reader still may find your writing hard to follow. When I talk about sentences flowing together, what I'm referring to is *coherence*, which is not the same thing as *cohesion*. I distinguish the two in this way: In a cohesive piece of writing, the sentences fit together one by one in the way that pieces of a jigsaw puzzle do. In a coherent text, all the sentences add up to a whole in the way that all the pieces in a puzzle make the picture shown on the box. There are several strategies you can use to improve the coherence of your paragraphs. The most powerful of these is known as the "old-to-new" sequence.

LINK SENTENCES WITH THE OLD-TO-NEW SEQUENCE

Except for your paragraphs' topic sentences, try to begin each sentence with "old information" (i.e., information the reader likely already knows). Such old information may be considered old because readers have just read it in a preceding sentence or paragraph, or it may be familiar to them because it's general knowledge. Then, as for your "new information" (i.e., information the reader likely doesn't already know), you can put it at the end of the sentence.

The reason behind this writing strategy is an understanding of how people learn something new: connecting new information to something you *already* know makes it easier to process and recall later. Plus, most readers prefer to read what's familiar before what's novel and harder to grasp quickly. When you use the old-to-new sequence consistently, your paragraphs will be coherent.

Let's look at an example of what the old-to-new sequence could look like (<u>underlined</u> text is new; **bolded** text is old):

Given the increased variety of support and widened reach of care available to returning American military veterans, <u>their involvement in Department of Veterans Affairs (VA) treatment programs is relatively low.</u> **This low participation rate**, coupled with an increased rate of suicide among veterans, signals that many are not receiving the help they need from the <u>VA's resources.</u> **The Department's resources** are opt-in, meaning veterans must actively seek them out. <u>There are, however, many factors that prevent veterans from seeking care.</u> **These include**, but are not limited to:

- general distrust of mental health professionals;
- lack of awareness of mental health conditions;
- belief their condition is not severe enough to warrant treatment; or
- belief they will be viewed negatively, as weak, or as out of control.

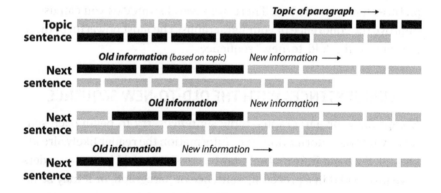

Notice how old information is introduced in a phrase, a subordinate clause, and even the repetition of a word (or its pronoun *these*). The most important thing to remember is that your old information shouldn't take up too much space in the sentence. Some writers repeat far too much, perhaps because they feel more information will lead to better understanding. Try not to do that. The bulk of your sentences should be devoted to new information. Note, too, that there isn't a single transitional phrase. No *in addition* or *moreover*. No *on the contrary* or *consequently*.

Let's look at another example:

> While all people aged 60 and above are eligible to receive certain in-home services, most of these services are not entitlements, meaning not all who would benefit from them will receive them. Congress provided approximately $1.2 billion in fiscal years 2013 and 2014 for grants to states to provide in-home services, though in most states demand outstripped the funding.

The sentence that introduces the amount of money Congress appropriated for this program seems out of place because it lacks any explicit relationship to the old information. Readers need that old information to orient themselves to new information. Notice how much more clearly the passage reads after the addition of a short "orienting phrase" (in **bold**):

> While <u>all people aged 60 and above</u> are eligible to receive certain in-home services, most of these services are not entitlements, meaning not all who would benefit from them will receive them. **To meet the needs of this vulnerable population**, Congress provided approximately $1.2 billion in fiscal years 2013 and 2014 for grants to states to provide in-home services, though in most states demand outstripped the funding.

LINK SENTENCES BY REPEATING KEY WORDS AND PHRASES THROUGHOUT THE PARAGRAPH

Many of us have been trained to avoid repeating terms because doing so risks boring readers. But readers frequently skim rather than read sentence by sentence. Using the same term throughout a passage helps readers understand that various pieces of information in a paragraph are related. Be careful with this technique, though. Too much repetition, or repetition of nonessential information, distracts the reader and makes a paragraph dull, wordy, and redundant.

Two important uses of repetition are for accuracy and as a transition.

1. Use repetition when needed for accuracy

Changing key words or phrases can confuse readers who wonder whether the change denotes a difference in meaning.

> *Draft*: Under the new health care law, hospitals are required to ensure doctors comply with new rules and regulations governing outpatient care. If the hospital finds health care professionals are not complying, they are required to report those physicians and/or issue fines.

> *Revision*: Under the new health care law, hospitals are required to ensure physicians comply with new rules and regulations governing outpatient care. If the hospital finds they are not complying, the hospitals are required to report them and/or issue fines.

Notice how confusing the variation in terms can be. Is a *doctor* the same as a *health care professional*? Aren't nurses and others who administer care also considered health care professionals? Notice in the revision how easy it is to keep track of who is who when we use *they* and *them* to refer to *physicians*.

2. Use repetition to relate sentences logically

Repeating a key word or phrase from one sentence to another helps the reader understand the relationship between the two sentences. For example:

> The **Department of Defense (DOD) and the VA** are spending substantial *time, money, and effort* on the management of post-traumatic stress disorder (PTSD) in service members and veterans. *Those efforts* have resulted in a <u>variety of programs and services</u> for the prevention and diagnosis of, treatment for, rehabilitation of, and research on PTSD and its comorbidities. Nevertheless, **neither department** knows with certainty whether <u>those many programs and services</u> are successful in reducing the prevalence of PTSD in service members or veterans and in improving their lives.

WHEN ALL ELSE FAILS, LINK SENTENCES WITH TRANSITIONAL WORDS AND PHRASES

Transitional words and phrases lead the reader from one idea to another. They enhance the coherence of your writing by signaling to the reader how an idea logically connects to the preceding one. Notice how the simple addition of a few sentence-starting transitions (shown in **bold** below) makes clear the connection between sentences:

> We employed several methodologies to check for compliance among the four military services with the DOD's new requirements regarding separating service members. **First,** to analyze the extent to which the DOD and the different military services are able to identify the number of enlisted service members who were administratively separated because of a "nondisability mental condition," we reviewed various documents, including the DOD's policy on the use of codes to track specific types of separations. **Second,** we interviewed DOD and military service officials to understand the type of tracking conducted and whether they maintained data on separations for nondisability mental conditions, as well as any requirements related to tracking such separations. **In addition,** we reviewed the DOD's and the military services' separation policies to identify requirements for separating service members for nondisability mental conditions, how these requirements have evolved, and whether the requirements have been consistently applied.

You will find a list of frequently used transitional words and phrases in table 8.1. Be careful with transitions, though. Some writers try to fake coherence by lacing their prose with conjunctions such as *thus, therefore,* and *however,* regardless of whether they signal logical connections. Experienced writers, on the other hand, use transitional words and phrases to signpost the logical flow of ideas. They are especially careful not to overuse words and phrases such as *in addition, and, also, moreover, another*—words that say, simply, *Here's one more thing.* Overuse of *in addition* may mean that you are stringing together data.

When you express cause and effect, use *therefore* or *consequently* to wind up a line of reasoning. But avoid using words like these more than a few times per page. Overuse of the transition word *however* may mean that you have not thought through the point you're trying to communicate. "Don't start a sentence with 'however'" says William Zinsser, author of *On Writing Well*: "it hangs there like a wet dishrag. And don't end with 'however'—by that time it has lost its howeverness. Put it as early as you reasonably can. Its abruptness then becomes a virtue."[1]

TABLE 8.1. Frequently used transitional words and phrases

Addition	further, also, in addition, next, furthermore, moreover, additionally
Cause and effect	thus, as a result, therefore, consequently, because, accordingly, hence, subsequently
Comparison	similarly, likewise, in the same way
Contrast	but, yet, however, nevertheless, in contrast, on the other hand, on the contrary, instead, actually
Illustration and elaboration	for example, specifically, in particular, more precisely, in fact, indeed, more specifically, namely, that is, for instance, in other words
Numerical order	first, second, third; first, then, finally
Time	after, before, next, at the same time, currently, earlier

CHAPTER 9

Clear and Concise Sentences

Do me a favor. As you read the sentence below, try to picture who is doing what:

> The potential for inconsistent penalty administration within a decentralized management structure is exacerbated by the complexity of the penalty process within the IRS.

What did you picture? Nothing? If so, that's a problem because readers understand stories better when they can picture them as they're reading. It's that simple. Unfortunately, you don't have to look hard to find policy briefs on the internet that are riddled with sentences like the one above. Why do you think that is? It's doubtful that a writer *wanted* to write a sentence so difficult to understand. What's more likely is that whoever wrote this sentence tried hard to write it well but struggled with what Harvard psychology professor Steven Pinker calls "the curse of knowledge." The curse of knowledge means that the more you know about something, the less clearly you tend to write about it. That's because once we human beings learn something, it's difficult for us to imagine what it was like *not* to know that thing. "I think the curse of knowledge is the chief contributor to opaque writing," Pinker explained in a 2015 lecture. "It simply doesn't occur to the writer that readers haven't learned their jargon, don't seem to know the intermediate steps that seem to them to be too obvious to mention, and can't visualize a scene currently in the writer's mind's eye. And so the writer doesn't bother to explain the jargon, or spell out the logic, or supply the concrete details—even when writing for professional peers."[1]

When readers encounter a sentence like the one above about the IRS, they probably won't stop reading to decipher it. Some readers may blame themselves at first for not understanding what the sentence means. They may think they missed something, so they'll reread the sentence. But they won't keeping doing that for long. Soon enough, they'll blame the writer. They'll grow doubtful of what the writer has to say, which will make it difficult to persuade them that the policy story is worthy of their attention.

If you want your public policy writing to matter, you *must* tell stories your reader can follow without getting lost. Psychologists and neurologists have known for quite some time that humans are primed for telling and understanding narratives about people acting in the world. It's how our species has survived for so many thousands of years.

Imagine if that weren't true—just for a moment. Let's say, for example, that one of our distant ancestors was out for a walk along a river just as the sun was setting. He was minding his own business, taking in the pristine views of the countryside. Then, out of nowhere, a saber-toothed tiger sprung from the bushes. And let's say this ancestor of ours was fortunate enough to escape the tiger and make it back to the cave. I bet that once he calmed down, he told his friends and family all about what had happened. He probably concluded that we should be careful at sundown while walking along the river and that we should never let the beauty of the land distract us from checking our surroundings for predators. It's this kind of storytelling that passes wisdom down so that future generations might avoid making the same mistake.

Now imagine how quickly our species might have died out had our ancestor buried the point of his story in unclear subjects and verbs that conveyed no action. What if, instead of telling a story in which he made it clear how to avoid being eaten, he said something like this:

The potential for untimely expiration by means of predator attack is exacerbated by the inability to maintain ocular awareness during twilight while in close proximity to a natural flowing watercourse.

And what if we took that turgid sentence about the IRS and rewrote it thus:

The IRS likely administers penalties inconsistently because it has a decentralized management structure and a complex penalty process.

Was that easier to picture? So much easier, right? And it's not even that hard to make such revisions after you learn how to harness the power of the "sentence core." According to Joseph M. Williams and Gregory G. Colomb, authors of the highly recommended *Style: Lessons in Clarity and Grace,* the sentence core comprises two parts: the *actor* and the *action.*[2] The relative strength of a sentence core depends on the answers to four questions:

1. Is the subject of the sentence close to the verb?
2. Is the subject something the reader can easily picture?
3. Does the verb show the reader action?
4. Are the subject and verb near the beginning of the sentence?

The answer to all four questions should be an emphatic YES. The difference between a strong sentence core and a weak sentence core is like the difference between a stop sign and a doctor's signature.

ENSURE THE SENTENCE'S ACTOR AND ACTION CAN BE FOUND IN THE SENTENCE CORE

A subject (or actor) can be an individual person; a program, agency, or political party; or even a concept—like the "broken windows" theory of community policing. The more abstract a subject gets, however, the more difficult it will be for a reader to picture.

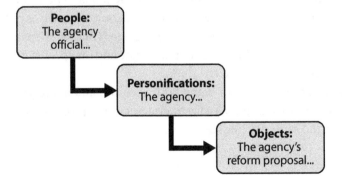

On the subject of writing about people, I'd like to plug a fabulous resource I found called *A Progressive's Style Guide*. It was published by SumOfUs, a nonprofit organization that advocates for social change in the United States. In the introduction to the guide, the authors make a key point about the language we use to describe the people we write about in public policy: "Language can build bridges and change minds. By acknowledging the ability of language to shape and reflect reality, progressive campaigns can become more powerful vehicles for social change, inclusion, and justice."[3] Even if you don't identify as a progressive, there are plenty of worthwhile lessons to take from this style guide that can help you ensure your writing is as accurate *and* appropriate as possible.

Let's look at an example that shows what a difference accurate *and* appropriate language can make. Imagine that you have been asked to analyze data on employment and earnings from the American Community Survey. Specifically, you've been asked to compare what you find across demographic groups for the city of Chicago. It's possible, if you're not careful, to end up writing a key finding that reads something like this:

> The data suggest Blacks and Hispanics work as hard as Whites in Chicago, but their work is not as valuable.

Let's be charitable here and give the writer the benefit of the doubt. I'll bet the writer did not intend to say that Black and Hispanic people in Chicago are not as valuable as White people. We also have no idea what the writer meant by "hard." Does that refer to the number of hours worked or to how physically demanding the job is? The last problem we have here is that the sentence takes the people themselves out of the message when it refers to people as categories (Blacks, Hispanics, and Whites). Not only is the sentence inaccurate and inappropriate, but it's also unnecessarily abstract.

With the twin goals of being both accurate and appropriate—and ensuring your writing is as easy to understand as possible—what if we rewrote the sentence like so:

> The data suggest Black and Hispanic residents of Chicago work about the same number of hours each week as their White neighbors, but their work is compensated, on average, at a lower rate.

Is this more appropriate? Definitely. We're talking about people—residents and neighbors—not categories. But is it accurate? Yes, actually. By specifying what *hard* and *valuable* mean as they relate to employment and earnings, we've made the sentence more accurate and true to the original data. When trying to find the right way to describe people, I keep four points in mind when writing with people-first language:

1. The focus should be on people, not on the categories you may sort them into.
2. If you're not sure what term to use, ask the people you're writing about how they prefer to identify themselves.
3. Specificity is your friend. Be as specific as you can be.
4. Recognize that language is not only dynamic and informed by culture, but it also depends on context and audience.

Now that we've got a clearer sense of how we might write about people effectively, let's turn to verbs. This is where things get slippery. Let's take a closer look at the IRS example. Pay special attention to the subject (underlined) and the verb (**bolded**):

> The potential for inconsistent penalty administration within a decentralized management structure **is** exacerbated by the complexity of the penalty process within the IRS.

Because the writer used a to-be verb (is), the action of the sentence had to go somewhere. Where it went was into three nouns: administration, management, and penalty. We call this kind of noun a nominalization, which means a noun derived from a verb or adjective. *Administration* comes from the verb *administer, management* comes from *manage,* and *penalty* comes from *penalize.*

Because the action of the sentence is hidden in nominalizations, the subject of the sentence becomes an abstract concept (potential).

And when a sentence has a to-be verb, several nominalizations, and an abstract concept for a subject, the writer needs several prepositions (italicized below) to tie all the different parts of speech into a complete sentence:

> The potential *for* inconsistent penalty administration *within* a decentralized management structure is exacerbated *by* the complexity *of* the penalty process *within* the IRS.

Now, because all this unnecessary complexity is the result of using the wrong verb, we need to strengthen the sentence by finding a recognizable subject and verb that show action. We can find that action in the nominalizations:

> The IRS **likely administers** penalties inconsistently because it has a decentralized management structure and a complex penalty process.

There are four things I'd like you to notice about this revision. First, it's much easier to process mentally. Second, we didn't need to get rid of all the nominalizations. Two of the three were helpful, in fact. Third, the revision is shorter (18 words versus 23). That's because we were able to delete the prepositions stringing the nominalizations together. Last, though certainly not least, we didn't lose *any* of the information. It was easy to keep it in because when readers understand who is doing what, they can incorporate new information into the frame created by the sentence core.

Nominalization might sound like grammatical jargon, but it's actually a useful term. Here are some examples of common nominalizations used in public policy writing:

VERB → NOMINALIZATION		ADJECTIVE → NOMINALIZATION	
discover	discovery	careless	carelessness
move	movement	difficult	difficulty
resist	resistance	different	difference
react	reaction	elegant	elegance
fail	failure	applicable	applicability
refuse	refusal	intense	intensity

It's important to note that nominalizations are not always bad. Writers rely on nouns to name things, after all. For example, when you describe something as an "agreement," you are using a nominalization: *agreement* is nominalized from the verb *agree*. There is nothing unclear about *agreement* when you use it to name a thing, such as a contract. Furthermore, in following the old-to-new strategy of sequencing information, you can use a nominalization as the subject of a sentence that refers to a previous sentence:

These *arguments* all depend on an incomplete data set.

This *decision* could result in an unnecessary burden on recipients.

In addition, you can use a nominalization to refer to an often-repeated concept. In the following sentences, the nominalizations name concepts that we refer to repeatedly. Rather than spell out a familiar concept in a full clause each time we mention it, we contract it into a noun. In these cases, the abstractions often become virtual actors:

The Equal Rights *Amendment* featured prominently in last week's presidential debate.

The last thing I'll say about ensuring your sentence core contains the most important information is to limit the length of "orienting language" at the beginning of your sentences. You can use orienting language at the beginning of a sentence to tell the reader when or where something happened. Orienting language can also be used to show purpose or attribution.

- *Time*: <u>From 2010 through 2012,</u> the DOD developed criteria for evaluating its transition assistance programs.
- *Place*: <u>In both Chicago and New York,</u> the VA has well-established hospitals that offer inpatient care for various mental conditions.
- *Purpose*: The trend has been to discharge service members who show signs of battle fatigue. <u>To cope with this trend,</u> the VA has had to improve outreach in its warrior transition programs.

- *Attribution*: <u>According to one official we spoke to,</u> there are many reasons why a program may choose not to collect performance data.

PLACE THE VERB NEAR THE SUBJECT

"Nothing more frustrates understanding," writes Richard Lauchman in *Plain Style*, than "verbs that are 'politely late' to the party. Always organize sentences so that the verb appears as close as possible to the subject."[4] This guidance is based on the limitations of short-term memory, which we rely on when reading. If you write a sentence in which the subject is far from the verb or the verb far from the object, it may be harder for the reader to follow. By the time readers reach the verb, they may have forgotten the subject, and by the time they reach the object, they may have forgotten the verb. Readers may have to reread a sentence when more than seven words come between the subject and the verb. In the following examples, the subject is <u>underlined</u>, and the verb is **bolded**.

> *Sentence 1*: <u>Enrollment in the program</u>, increasing from 120,480 veterans in 1994 to 240,487 in 1998, **doubled**.

> *Sentence 2*: From 1994 to 1998, <u>veteran enrollment in the program</u> **doubled**, increasing from 120,480 to 240,487.

Why is Sentence 1 more difficult to understand than Sentence 2? The answer is simple: structure. In Sentence 1, the subject (Enrollment in the program) is followed by a ten-word phrase before we come to the verb (doubled). As readers, we're held in a state of uncertainty about what the subject is doing or what the sentence is about until we get to the verb. In awaiting the arrival of the verb, the reader can't recognize what's significant about the intervening words. In Sentence 2, because the subject and verb are close together (<u>veteran employment in the program</u> **doubled**), the reader can quickly process the content.

BONUS TIP: USE THE ACTIVE VOICE

You can make your writing clearer and more direct if you use the active voice and avoid using the passive voice. If it's been a while since you thought about passive voice, here's a quick reminder: The subject of a sentence written in the active voice is the doer of the action (the actor). The subject of a sentence written in the passive voice is acted upon by the object of the sentence. For example:

Active voice: The legislator criticized the agency's position.

Passive voice: The agency's position was criticized by the legislator.

Passive voice has a bad reputation—and for good reason. Writing in the passive voice can make writers (1) use subjects that are *not* actors or (2) omit important actors altogether. "Often, in a sentence constructed in the passive voice," writes Benjamin Dreyer, Random House's copy chief, "the actor is omitted entirely. Sometimes this is done in an attempt to call attention to a problem without laying blame ('The refrigerator door was left open') and sometimes, in weasel-like fashion, to avoid taking responsibility: 'Mistakes were made,' for instance, which, uttered on various occasions by various Bushes, may well be the motto of that political dynasty."[5]

Readers of English instinctively look for the actor in the subject position of a sentence. If the subject does not name an actor, readers may judge the sentence to be unclear, indirect, and difficult to process. Most readers prefer to read the active voice, especially in policy writing, because the active voice conveys information more clearly and concisely than the passive voice. "The difference," William Zinsser writes, "between an active-verb style and a passive-verb style—in clarity and vigor—is the difference between life and death for a writer."[6]

From as early as I can remember, I've been told by English teachers that I shouldn't use passive voice—ever. This rule, like many "rules" in English, isn't a rule at all. Sometimes, sentences written in passive voice create a clearer sentence than one written in the active voice. For example, passive voice can allow you to use a subject that is an actor when using the active voice would force you to use a subject that is not an actor. Here are four other situations in which passive voice is appropriate:

1. *The actor is unknown*: The veterans' claims were misplaced, and the veterans were left on the agency's wait list for almost two years before someone located the claims.
2. *It is not important who the actor is*: The new information technology infrastructure was completed early and under budget.
3. *The receiver of the action, not the actor, needs to be emphasized*: Numerous veterans were sent inaccurate payments.
4. *The focus needs to be kept on the same actor over two sentences (like with the old-to-new sequence)*: Veterans applying for disability benefits must first fill out an electronic application on the VA's website. In collecting evidence needed to justify their claim, veterans are encouraged by the VA to consult with their primary care providers.

Before we move on to the next chapter, let's take a quick look at an example (from Williams and Colomb's *Style*) of how using nominalizations and passive voice can have real-world implications.

In 1985, the Government Accounting Office—now the Government Accountability Office—reported on why fewer than half of automobile owners who received a recall letter from their car's manufacturer complied with the instructions in the letter. The reason was that many owners could not understand what they were being asked to do. The following is an example of how writers can simultaneously meet legal requirements while unwittingly (I hope, anyway!) ignoring ethical obligations. Look at this gem:

A defect which involves the possible failure of a frame support plate may exist on your vehicle. This plate (front suspension pivot bar support plate) connects a portion of the front suspension to the vehicle frame, and its failure could affect vehicle directional control, particularly during heavy brake application. In addition, your vehicle may require adjustment service to the hood secondary catch system. The secondary catch may be misaligned so that the hood may not be adequately restrained to prevent hood fly-up in the event the primary

latch is inadvertently left unengaged. Sudden hood fly-up beyond
the secondary catch while driving could impair driver visibility. In
certain circumstances, occurrence of either of the above conditions
could result in vehicle crash without prior warning.[7]

The author of this letter nominalized all the verbs that might make a
reader anxious, made most of the other verbs passive, and then deleted
just about every reference to the actors, particularly the manufacturer.
If you were to revise some of these sentences to make them clearer
and more concise, one sentence, according to Williams, would surely
read, "If you brake hard and the plate fails, you will not be able to steer
your car."

Clear writing can save lives. Simple as that.

CHAPTER 10

Eleven Strategies for Ruthlessly Pruning Needless Words

Years ago, when I was working for the Government Accountability Office in its Chicago field office, I lived over the Wisconsin border and commuted to the office via train a few days per week. Even though it was long ago, I can still remember the announcement that would blare across the platform as my train pulled into the station:

> Metra commuters, your attention, please. An inbound train to Chicago is now arriving in your station. For your safety, please stand behind the yellow line until the train has come to a complete stop before boarding the train.

That announcement always bothered me because it was such a waste of breath. Allow me to explain why: *Metra commuters, your attention, please.* (No problem yet.) *An inbound train to Chicago* (As opposed to an *inbound* train *from* Chicago?) *is now arriving* (It is? I was wondering what the flashing lights and clanging bells were all about.) *in your station.* (I'm glad I'm not waiting for a train that's going to stop in someone else's station. By the way, is it really *my* station?) *For your safety, please stand behind the yellow line* (Shouldn't I be concerned for everyone's safety? Maybe Metra is trying to appeal to my selfish inclinations?) *until the train has come to a complete stop* (As opposed to a partial stop? Is there such a thing?) *before boarding the train.* (Enough people must have tried to board the train while it was still moving that Metra felt compelled to issue this warning.)

This problem of using too many words is one that most of us deal with in college when trying to impress our professors. It is engrained in us that longer papers are better than shorter ones and that bigger, fancier words are better than smaller, simpler ones. I once had a professor say that the way he graded papers was by throwing them down the stairs of his house. The heavier papers with more pages would make it to the bottom step. Those papers received the highest grades. The rest got lower grades. He was kidding, of course, but he told us that if we wanted to pass his course, we would need to write until our "fingers bleed!"

When I was in graduate school at the University of Chicago, I took great pride in using words that other people might not know: *interstice* and *bifurcation* and *imbricate* and *hermeneutics*. Using such words was like donning mental armor that made me feel smarter, like I belonged. If someone did not understand what I wrote, I convinced myself, they must not have been as smart as I was. Oh how wrong I was.

Steven Pinker, author of *The Sense of Style*, studies both the science of cognitive psychology—how the brain processes language, how we associate words with meanings—and the art of language. In a 2014 interview, he laid out the reasons that graduate students are often ineffective writers. When you enter graduate school, Pinker said, "Your estimate of the breadth of the knowledge of the people you are writing for gets radically miscalibrated. Highly idiosyncratic ideas are discussed as if they are common knowledge, and you lose the sense of how tiny a club you have joined." In addition, Pinker continued, "You're in terror of being judged naive and unprepared, and so you signal in your writing that you're a member of this esoteric club."[1]

"Simpler writing is easier to process, and studies have demonstrated that processing fluency is associated with a variety of positive dimensions," including "higher judgments of truth," confidence, frequency, fame, and even "liking," according to a study conducted by Daniel M. Oppenheimer, a professor of psychology at Princeton University. In the article he wrote about his findings, with the tongue-in-cheek title "Consequences of Erudite Vernacular Utilized Irrespective of Necessity," Oppenheimer concludes that "overly complex texts caused readers to have negative evaluations of those texts and the associated authors, especially if the complexity was unnecessary."[2] What this means for us policy analysts is that we must fight the urge to "utilize erudite vernac- ular irrespective of necessity," and we must call it out as unhelpful and potentially exclusionary.

Before I show you 11 ways of pruning your writing, I'd like to note that it is possible for you to revise the examples I use in this chapter even more radically than I did. And you would be right to do so. If I had completely rewritten every example, however, I would only show you that it is possible to rethink the whole idea of a sentence—something that I cannot easily teach—and at the end of the chapter, you would probably still not understand how I did what I did. So, for pedagogi- cal reasons, I stayed as close as I could to the original content of each drafted sentence.

1. DON'T USE A FANCY WORD WHEN A SIMPLE ONE WILL DO

There is a common word for every fancy one. When you use the common word, you rarely lose anything important. Replacing unnec- essarily formal words with more common ones will make your writing sharper and more direct, and your readers will appreciate the result.

Draft: Pursuant to the recent memorandum issued November 29, 2014, because of financial exigencies, it is incumbent upon us all to endeavor to make maximal utilization of electronic communication in lieu of personal visitation.

Revision: As the memo issued on November 29, 2014, said, to save money you should use email as much as you can instead of making personal visits.

2. WHEN POSSIBLE, COMPRESS SEVERAL WORDS INTO A WORD OR TWO

Avoid restating words and phrases that do not add meaning, and avoid using excessive words that you could remove without losing meaning. For example, instead of writing *the reason for, for the reason that, due to the fact that, in light of the fact that*, we could use *because*.

Draft: In light of the fact that the agency received funding cuts from 2003 through 2009, it did not have enough resources to complete its projects.

Revision: Because the agency received funding cuts . . .

Instead of writing *despite the fact that, regardless of the fact that,* or *notwithstanding the fact that,* we could use *although* or *even though.*

Draft: Despite the fact that the program's performance measures were calculated several times, serious errors crept into the findings.

Revision: Even though the program's performance measures . . .

Instead of writing *in the event that, if it should transpire/happen that,* or *under circumstances in which,* we could use *if.*

Draft: In the event that the program fails to meet certain standards, its funding may be cut.

Revision: If the program fails . . .

Instead of writing *on the occasion of, in a situation in which,* or *under circumstances in which,* we could use *when.*

Draft: In a situation in which a program does not detect fraudulent applications, the program may be required to develop a more formal application procedure.

Revision: When a program detects fraud . . .

Instead of writing *as regards, in reference to, with regard to, concerning the matter of,* or *where x is concerned,* we could use *about.*

Draft: The first observation I would like to make is in reference to contingency funds.

Revision: The first observation I would like to make is about contingency funds.

Instead of writing *it is crucial that, it is necessary that, there is a need for, it is important that, it is incumbent upon,* or *it cannot be avoided,* we could use *must* or *should.*

> *Draft*: There is a need for more careful inspection of all teacher preparation programs.

> *Revision*: We must inspect all teacher preparation programs more carefully.

Instead of writing *is able to, is in a position to, has the opportunity to, has the capacity for,* or *has the ability to,* we could use *can.*

> *Draft*: We are in a position to make a recommendation that will improve the program.

> *Revision*: We can make a recommendation that will improve the program.

> *Further revision*: We can recommend an improvement for the program.

Instead of writing *it is possible that, there is a chance that, it could happen that,* or *the possibility exists for,* we could use *may.*

> *Draft*: It is possible that nothing will come of these findings.

> *Revision*: Nothing may come of these findings.

Instead of writing *prior to* or *in anticipation of,* we could use *before.*

> *Draft*: Prior to the expiration of the enrollment period, all forms must be submitted.

> *Revision*: Before the enrollment period expires . . .

Table 10.1 has some more common examples you may find helpful.

TABLE 10.1. Suggested revisions for wordy phrases

Wordy phrase	Alternative
a sufficient amount of	enough
come to the conclusion	conclude
consensus of opinion	consensus
cooperated together	cooperated
for the purpose of	to, for
if the conditions are such that	if
in order to	to
in spite of the fact that	although
is in a position to	can
located within	in
necessary requirement	required
subsequent to	after

Back when I was teaching policy writing at Johns Hopkins University, one of my students showed me a sentence he had written using nearly all the wordy and redundant phrases I had showed the class how to prune. Here's what he wrote:

> A sufficient amount of people have come to the conclusion that despite the fact that they are located within the same building and cooperated together in order to gain a consensus of opinion for the purpose of writing if the conditions are such that prior to attaining knowledge, they are in a position to have a necessary requirement in the event that a lack thereof of the aforementioned knowledge is existent in spite of the fact that, and due to the fact of learning.

"Put super simply," he told me, "it means that people come here to learn how to write better, but they don't know that yet."

3. DELETE "DOUBLE WORDS"

The English language has a long tradition of unnecessarily doubling words. Among common pairs are these:

- *full* and *complete*
- *each* and *every*
- *first* and *foremost*
- *any* and *all*
- *could* and *potentially*

Here's the secret to avoiding double words: pick one and delete the other.

4. PRUNE REDUNDANT MODIFIERS

Get rid of words implied by other words. *Finish* implies *complete*, for example, so writing *completely finish* is redundant. Here are a few more examples:

- *Basic* implies *fundamental*, so *basic fundamentals* is redundant.
- *Important* implies *essentials*, so *important essentials* is redundant.
- *Final* implies *outcome*, so *final outcome* is redundant.

Other examples include *true facts, future plans, consensus of opinion, sudden crisis, terrible tragedy, end result, direct confrontation, exact same, mutual cooperation,* and *initial preparation.*

And here's an egregious example of redundant modifiers in action:

Draft: The agencies have developed a *joint, cooperative* contingency plan for *anticipating unexpected* demands on their capacity and resources before all *new upgrades* can be made to their *core, essential* systems.

Notice how much better it is when we drop the redundancies:

> *Revision*: The agencies have developed a contingency plan to deal with unexpected demands on their resources before all upgrades can be made to their core systems.

5. DELETE "EMPTY NOUNS" AND OVERUSED MODIFIERS

Some modifiers are what we might call "verbal tics." That is, they are words we use almost unconsciously. You can usually omit these. They include *really, basically, definitely, actually, virtually, particular, different*, and *specific*. For example:

> *Draft*: While this is generally seen as a logical approach that provides certain advantages, it has also practically reduced the agency's ability to control its staff's various day-to-day activities.

Look how much clearer it reads when we drop the empty nouns and overused modifiers:

> *Revision*: While some see this as a logical approach that provides advantages, it has also reduced the agency's ability to control its staff's day-to-day activities.

6. BE CAUTIOUS WITH ADVERBS

In his book on writing, famed author of horror Stephen King cautions writers that "the road to hell is paved with adverbs."[3] If that helps you err on the side of caution when using adverbs, that's fine. Commit it to memory. If you're like me and appreciate a more nuanced approach, rest assured that while you can omit most adverbs without losing meaning, there are plenty of adverbs you should use in policy writing.

Probably the most egregious adverbs add redundancy. For example, if you were to write "constricted tightly," the adverb *tightly* doesn't add anything to the sentence because *constricted* already means "to make narrower" or "to tighten." When you come across such adverbs in your writing, ask yourself whether the adverb is covered by the definition of the word it's modifying. If you can delete the adverb without changing the meaning of the sentence, do it.

Other kinds of adverbs help hide the fact that you're using the wrong verb. You could write, for instance, that a government agency "went too quickly" through the required process for procuring some new piece of equipment. Or you could say it "sped" through the process. If you can think of a verb that means the same thing as the verb plus adverb, go with the stand-alone verb.

You can also ditch adverbs that serve as intensifiers—*completely, totally, absolutely*. These sorts of adverbs are generally overused and don't add much to a sentence. So too are adverbs that qualify the degree of an action—like *somewhat* or *moderately*. Writing that a regulation was "somewhat difficult to understand" can make you seem timid. Don't get me wrong, though. There are times when you *need* to convey caution and uncertainty. All I ask is that you make sure you're doing it intentionally and for good reason. The best advice I can give you for how to avoid unnecessary adverbs is to practice. Condition yourself to avoid them in your writing. This will take time and patience. Even after years of professional writing, useless adverbs still slip past me all the time. If you find you cannot stop yourself from using them, dedicate some time during the revision and editing process to finding and deleting them.

On the other hand, adverbs that add clarity or improve the flow of your writing are useful tools. For example, adverbs of time, place, and manner clarify when, where, and how something happened. If you think an adverb is working for you, that's great. Keep it.

Another way to learn the difference between useful and unnecessary adverbs is from the supreme writing teacher: reading. Read great books, magazines, newspapers, and blogs. Read great sentences until you can tell when one isn't. Read great paragraphs until their rhythms get stuck in your head. Only by reading can you know when an adverb belongs in a sentence and when it should be cut.

7. AVOID UNNECESSARILY RESTATING WORDS AND PHRASES

As we have seen, repeating key words and phrases is a way to let our reader know that the premise set forth in a topic sentence is supported in the sentences that follow. We do not, however, want to restate words or phrases that do not add meaning or that could be removed without losing meaning.

It is just as important to let the context establish the basis for our successive statements. If you properly identify the subject in the first sentence, it may be preferable to use a generic synonym or a pronoun in the second sentence, such as referring to the Social Security Administration as "the agency" or referring to "the former" of two already-named parties. Take this example:

> *Draft*: Child Protective Services agencies collect information about children who are maltreated—including children who have died from maltreatment—and the circumstances surrounding the maltreatment to aid efforts that prevent maltreatment.

The writer here has overused the word *maltreatment*. The writer was probably more concerned with being accurate than being concise. Here is a revision:

> *Revision*: To aid in prevention efforts, Child Protective Services agencies collect information about children who are maltreated—including children who have died—and the circumstances surrounding the maltreatment.

"Including children who have died" may not be an accurate rephrasing, though, if Child Protective Services only collects information on children who die because of maltreatment, as opposed to those who die because of accident or illness. A simple fix would be to fold (1) those children who are maltreated into (2) those who die as a result of their maltreatment:

> *Revision*: To aid prevention efforts, Child Protective Services agencies collect information about children who are harmed by or die from maltreatment.

8. MINIMIZE THE USE OF PREPOSITIONAL PHRASES

What do you think when you read this sentence?

Draft: In our interviews with officials in eight states, most could not accurately determine, based on the general definition in the law, which of their teachers met the new federal requirements.

How about now?

Revision: In eight states, most officials we interviewed could not determine which of their teachers met the new federal requirements.

The first sentence has 6 prepositional phrases and 30 words; the second has 2 prepositional phrases and 19 words.

Besides length, what's the difference? A well-structured sentence quickly directs the reader toward a main point—that is, *Who is doing what?* As we've seen, a sentence with too many prepositional phrases probably has a weak sentence core, which can leave the reader feeling lost at sea. If a sentence has more than three prepositional phrases— fronted by *in, with, on, of,* etc.—consider whether the reader might have difficulty focusing on your main point. The solution? Strengthen your sentence cores!

9. COMBINE SENTENCES TO AVOID REPEATING DETAILS

Rolling two sentences into one can sometimes push you to cut "filler" from an early draft. When some of the same information is repeated in consecutive sentences, that overlap may present you with an opportunity to combine them.

Draft: Over the last several years, the number of children for whom states receive reimbursements has declined. The average monthly number of children for whom states received reimbursements declined from about 200,000 in fiscal year 2007 to 169,000 in fiscal year 2013.

We could make this more concise by combining the two sentences:

Revision: Over the last several years, the average monthly number of children for whom states received reimbursements has declined from about 200,000 in fiscal year 2007 to 169,000 in fiscal year 2013.

Or we could write this:

Further revision: From fiscal year 2007 to 2013, the average monthly number of children for whom states received reimbursements declined from about 200,000 to 169,000.

The key to this technique is to identify the information the sentences share and then delete the redundant part from one of them. Then you can redraft a sentence with the unshared material that remains.

10. MAKE YOUR POINT AND MOVE ON

Policy analysts sometimes struggle so mightily to make their point that they unnecessarily repeat it. It's best to avoid that.

Draft: Due to the fact that more pension plans have become insolvent, the total amount of financial assistance the agency has provided has increased markedly in recent years. Overall, for fiscal year 2014, the agency provided $90 million in total financial assistance in order to help 45 insolvent plans cover pension benefits for about 49,000 plan participants. Generally, since 2001, the number of plans needing financial assistance has steadily increased, as has the total amount of assistance the agency has provided each year, drawing down the agency's insurance program funds. Moreover, the number of plans needing the agency's help has increased significantly in recent years, from 23 plans in fiscal year 2008 to 59 plans in fiscal year 2014. Likewise, the amount of annual assistance the agency has issued to plans has increased, from about $60 million in fiscal year 2008 to about $105 million in fiscal year 2014. (*148 words total*)

In addition to using wordy phrases (*Due to the fact that*) and needless transition words— *Overall, Generally, Moreover,* and *Likewise*—the author of this paragraph has repeated two points over and over: (1) the total amount of financial assistance the agency has provided increased markedly in recent years, and (2) the number of plans needing financial assistance has steadily increased. The writer made those two points three separate times. Notice what happens when we combine the two points and then present the data that prove them:

> *Revision*: Because more pension plans have become insolvent in recent years, the total amount of financial assistance the agency has provided has increased as well. The number of plans needing the agency's financial assistance has increased from 23 plans in fiscal year 2008 to 59 in fiscal year 2014. That year, the agency provided $105 million in total financial assistance—up from $60 million in fiscal year 2008—to help 59 insolvent plans cover pension benefits for about 49,000 plan participants. (*80 words total*)

The revised paragraph is more concise and easier to understand. In addition, it no longer needs those transition words binding redundant points.

11. USE HEDGING WORDS SPARINGLY

In today's world of six-second sound bites and rehearsed talking points, our institutional leaders perform verbal feats to escape having to tell us the truth—or even what they think. In his seminal text *On Writing Well*, William Zinsser tells us about "one classic offender" named Elliot Richardson, who held four cabinet posts in the 1970s. He's famous for serving as President Richard M. Nixon's attorney general and for resigning that position when the president asked him to fire those investigating the Watergate break-in. It's hard to choose the foggiest from Richardson's trove of equivocal statements, but Zinsser asks readers to consider this one: "And so, at last, I come to the one firm conviction that I mentioned at the beginning: it is that the subject is too new for final judgments."[4]

If every sentence we write expresses doubt, our writing will lack authority, and it won't inspire confidence, nor will it persuade skeptical readers. To paraphrase Zinsser, if we bob and weave like aging boxers, we won't inspire confidence. We won't deserve it either. We can do better. Here are some common hedging words to look out for:

- *Adverbs*: usually, often, sometimes, almost, virtually, possibly, allegedly, arguably, perhaps, apparently, in some ways, to a certain extent, somewhat, in some/certain respects
- *Adjectives*: most, many, some, a certain number of
- *Verbs and auxiliaries*: may, might, can, could, tend, suggest, imply

Don't get me wrong: Because hedging words qualify certainty, they are essential to the work we do as policy analysts. All I ask is that we use them sparingly. And don't hide behind them either. Save *would, should, could, may, might, can,* and other hedging words for situations involving real uncertainty.

BONUS TIP: LISTEN TO GEORGE ORWELL

"Political speech and writing," Orwell wrote in his famous essay on politics and the English language, "are largely the defense of the indefensible." To defend things like "the continuance of British rule in India, the Russian purges and deportations, the dropping of the atom bombs on Japan," writers had to use, he argued, language that was "too brutal for most people to face." So, instead, they chose vague euphemisms. *Pacification,* for example, sounded pleasant enough, but what that word really meant was "defenseless villages bombarded from the air, the inhabitants driven out into the countryside, the cattle machine-gunned, the huts set on fire with incendiary bullets." *Transfer of population* was something one could say instead of admitting that "millions of peasants are robbed of their farms and sent trudging along the roads with no more than they can carry." And if one *eliminates unreliable elements,* one need not mention the realities of people imprisoned "for years without trial, or shot in the back of the neck or sent to die of scurvy in Arctic lumber camps."[5]

Some institutions—especially governmental agencies—you'll likely come across in your work as a policy analyst do this sort of thing on purpose, hoping that you'll adopt their lexicon. Perhaps the most blatant example of this in recent memory is the language used at Guantanamo Bay detention facility. Since that facility opened its doors, military officials have developed their own lexicon to describe virtually everything that takes place there. For example, if a Guantanamo detainee attempts suicide, it's called "self-injurious behavior." Instead of shackles, military officials refer to the leg and wrist irons as "humane restraints." "Force-feeding" has been replaced with the clinical "enteral feeding," which replaced "assisted feeding." Even the use of "detainee" as opposed to "prisoner" and "detention facility" instead of "prison" was carefully thought out.

In 2014 Cori Crider, the legal director of Reprieve, an organization in the United Kingdom that was representing more than a dozen Guantanamo prisoners at the time, told Vice News that she believed the euphemisms used at the prison were chosen to "whitewash some of the more sordid things going on, although often the effect was just to make them more sinister and Orwellian." That same year Guantanamo Bay received the Vice News award for "best use of deflective phrasing."[6]

"What is above all needed," Orwell concluded, "is to let the meaning choose the word, and not the other way around."[7]

CHAPTER 11

Being Your Own Best Editor

Let's say you've written a draft of a policy memo, brief, article, or report. You've figured out what questions the reader needs answers to, found those answers, and positioned yourself as a helpful problem solver. After getting all that drafted, you may think you're done—or close to done. You are not, I'm afraid. The best writing—the writing that *matters*—is writing that has been through multiple rounds of revision, until every sentence sings.

But what do I mean when I talk about revision? It's not *just* about fixing typos and grammatical errors. Not by a long shot. Unfortunately, that seems to be what many people think revision is. Nancy Sommers, an education researcher at Harvard, once surveyed college students and professional writers about "what revision meant to them," and she found illuminating differences between the two groups. Two responses she recorded from students are striking. Revision is, they said,

- "Just using better words and eliminating words that are not needed. I go over and change words around."
- "Cleaning up the paper and crossing out. It is looking at something and saying, no that has to go, or no, that is not right."

Professional writers, on the other hand, defined revision as large-scale adjustments to argumentation and organization—not tinkering with words. Revision is, two respondents said,

- "On one level, finding the argument, and on another level, language changes to make the argument more effective."
- "A matter of looking at the kernel of what I have written, the

content, and then thinking about it, responding to it, making decisions, and actually restructuring it."[1]

Think of revision as an act of re-seeing. Does the story you're trying to tell

- answer the readers' questions clearly,
- help the readers achieve their goal, and
- provide enough evidence to convince them?

The biggest mistake you can make as a writer is to assume what you wrote in your first draft is good enough to release into the world.

BEFORE YOU REVISE

Set your writing aside for a while

Set your writing aside for a weekend, a day, or even just a couple of hours. Giving yourself this time allows you to refresh your perspective and separate yourself from your initial ideas and their organization.

Make a list of words you tend to use incorrectly or overuse

All writers, me included, have some words and phrases that (which?) always cause them to second-guess whether (weather?) they're (their?) using them correctly. If you know what your (you're?) troubling words are, you can use your word processor's search function to locate every variant of that word or phrase. In part V of this book, you'll find "A Style Guide for Public Policy Writing" that gives you tips on correctly using words that are commonly misused.

In addition to misusing words, all writers have words they overuse, also known as "crutch words." Once you spot these in a piece of writing, you won't be able to stop yourself from noticing how often you use them. Some commonly overused words and phrases that I routinely cut during revision are *however, indeed, in turn,* and *as a result.* I also struggle with what I call "filler words," such as *just, really, very, that, then,* and *even.* Usually I can delete these words without affecting the meaning of the sentence. The same is true for *rather, quite, in fact, surely, that said, actually,* and *of course.*

I'm not saying that we should never use our crutch words. It would be wrong to limit yourself in that way. Just make sure that when you use them, you *need* to use them. If you don't really need them—and you won't always need them—delete them. Trust me. Doing so will improve the readability of your writing.

For Microsoft Word users, there's a free Word Usage and Frequency add-in, but other, less technical online tools may also help, such as TextFixer.com's Online Word Counter or WriteWords' Word Frequency Counter. You can also use the Find function, although you must know what your crutch words are before you can find them.

Additionally, if you've got the funds and the inclination, you could buy a grammar checker. Some of my writer friends are fans of Grammarly. I prefer ProWritingAid. It's a plug-in I installed on Outlook, Chrome, and Microsoft Word, and it's incredibly helpful in pointing out grammar and spelling mistakes, as well as contextual errors like when a sentence is too long or repeats words or phrases. It doesn't magically make my writing perfect, but it definitely helps make it better.

Print out the document

Seeing your words on the printed page, as opposed to your computer screen, can help you spot obvious mistakes. I don't know the science behind this, but I'm convinced that revising on printed pages in my hands is different from revising an electronic document. I have friends who say that changing the font in the document can achieve a similar effect. It's about looking at your writing in a new way, with a different perspective.

You could also have your computer read your document aloud to you. If you're a Mac user, click the Apple logo at the top left of your screen, select System Preferences, click Accessibility, then click Speech; choose a System Voice and Speaking Rate you can tolerate, then select "Speak selected text when the key is pressed." If you want to change the keyboard combination, click Change Key and follow the directions. I prefer the combination Option + Esc. Once you've enabled your preferred shortcut keys, highlight any text (within any program) that you want read aloud. Then hit your shortcut keys and follow your words on-screen as your computer reads them aloud.

PC users can make use of Narrator, part of Window's Ease of Access Center. Press Windows + U and click Start Narrator. Since the program was designed for blind people, it will automatically read any text your mouse encounters. To turn this off, hit Control. To have Narrator read a paragraph, place your cursor at its beginning and press Caps Lock + I. To have Narrator read an entire page, press Caps Lock + U.

WHEN YOU REVISE

Focus first on "higher-order" concerns

As you're rereading your writing, have a blank piece of paper at hand or a blank document open on your computer, and write out these core elements:

- The real problem you address
- Your solution to the problem
- The required elements of your policy story
- The evidence you'll use to support your claims

Detailing these core elements will help you see your writing's basic structure and assess whether you are presenting a persuasive case for policy change. Once you've done that, read with an eye toward content, assertions, or logical leaps you may feel uncertain about. Are there questions left unanswered? Are there pieces of evidence that contradict or do not complement each other?

Read it out loud, sentence by sentence

By reading aloud what you've written, rather than scanning your words on a computer screen, you'll catch more problems and get a better feel for how everything flows. This is a good strategy for spotting run-on sentences, awkward phrases, and words that don't sound right for the context. It may also help to ask a friend to read your writing. What trips them up? What in your writing seems unclear to them? Be ready to listen graciously to their feedback. Table 11.1 provides a handy checklist for making sure you're following all the best practices featured in this book.

TABLE 11.1. A checklist to help you revise your writing

	Revision Question	✔
Content	Is the problem you're trying to solve clearly articulated?	☐
	Are you using the applicable elements of a finding to tell a story?	☐
	Condition: What's happening?	☐
	Criteria: What should be happening?	☐
	Cause: Why is the condition happening?	☐
	Effect: What will happen if the status quo is maintained? What will happen if your recommendations are implemented?	☐
	Are you providing enough context when presenting data?	☐
	Have you uncovered the *root cause* of the problem or challenge?	☐
	Have you explored the limitations of your findings or considered potential risks? Have you rebutted any possible opposition?	☐
	Do your recommendations arise logically from the evidence?	☐
	Are your recommendations feasible, cost-effective, and measurable?	☐
	Is the tone appropriate for your reader?	☐

TABLE 11.1. (*cont.*)

	Revision Question	✓
Clarity	Do you begin each paragraph with the main point (deductive structure)?	☐
	Does each of your paragraphs contain only one point (paragraph unity)?	☐
	Does every one of the sentences in each paragraph relate to or expand on its main point (paragraph coherence)?	☐
	Is the subject close to the verb and the subject-verb pairing (sentence core) close to the beginning of each sentence?	☐
	Are you writing about people whenever possible?	☐
	Are you using the old-to-new principle to structure your sentences?	☐
	Are you mostly writing in the active voice?	☐
	Do you avoid using jargon and define key terms throughout?	☐
	Do you use headings to signpost sections?	☐
	Does your structure and formatting conform to the reader's expectations?	☐
Concision	Is your written product as long as it needs to be but as short as it can be?	☐
	Have you read your product out loud?	☐
	Have you rooted out unnecessary weak verbs, nominalizations, and prepositional phrases?	☐
	Have you pruned any needless words ("double words," redundant or overused modifiers, empty nouns, and adverbs)?	☐
	Is your writing free of spelling, punctuation, and grammatical errors?	☐
	Does your writing contain sentence fragments, comma splices, or run-ons?	☐

CHAPTER 12

Quoting and Paraphrasing Sources Properly

To add credibility and authority to our policy writing, we integrate other people's words and ideas. When we do this, we must be careful not to pass off—intentionally or not—other people's words and ideas as our own. Doing so is plagiarism, and the University of Chicago considers "intellectual burglary" a breach of academic integrity. The penalties for obvious cases of plagiarism can be severe. To avoid plagiarizing other people's words and ideas, policy analysts must know how to quote and paraphrase properly.

WHETHER TO QUOTE FROM A SOURCE OR TO PARAPHRASE

Quote from a source when you need to

- present a specific take on a complex issue;
- compare one point to another—or critique or comment on a point;
- include moving, memorable, or significant language; or
- present a well-stated passage whose meaning might be lost if paraphrased.

Paraphrase when you need to

- describe an idea, not borrow someone's particular expression of it;

- express a key point more concisely; or
- change the structure or language of the original text.

HOW TO QUOTE EFFECTIVELY

To integrate a quotation into your policy story, you'll need to have two things:

- a *signal* that a quotation is coming (generally someone's name or other reference to them) and
- an *assertion* that explains the relevance of the quotation to your policy story.

Here is an example, with the signal in **bold** and the assertion in *italic*:

Unemployed older workers in our focus groups told us they wanted to return to work so they could pay for critical living expenses, including the cost of health care. Many said they had forgone seeking medical care or taking their prescribed medications because they could not afford them. *For example,* **one 56-year-old woman told us**, "I don't even want to go to the doctor to find out there's something wrong because then we can't afford to have it fixed."

And another example:

Results of recent academic studies contradict a popular notion that labor force participation by older workers diminishes employment opportunities for younger workers. One study, for example, shows that in numerous countries, over several decades, increased employment of older workers has not been associated with decreased employment of younger workers. The study also analyzed what happened to younger workers' employment rates in some European countries during specific time periods after increased numbers of older workers retired early. **The researchers concluded that** "the evidence suggests that greater labor force participation of older persons is associated with greater youth employment and with reduced youth unemployment." *In effect, the researchers found the opposite of* *what the popular notion of a zero-sum game would assume: they found that when older workers left their jobs to retire early, younger workers became unemployed.*

HOW TO PARAPHRASE EFFECTIVELY

Read the text you want to paraphrase several times until you understand it and can explain it in your own words. You may not need to paraphrase an entire passage. Look for the material that helps you make your point. Once you begin writing, try not to look at the original. Write the passage in your own words, and then review the original to see that you captured it accurately. If you find this difficult to do, it may be a sign that you don't yet fully understand the passage.

There is another, more specific strategy you can use to paraphrase effectively. First, consider the following passage from *Food Aid after Fifty Years: Recasting Its Role*:

> Traditional food aid programs were based on the assumption that declines in food availability cause food insecurity, including its most acute form: famine. Theoretical and empirical advances in the 1970s and 1980s demonstrated that while an inadequate overall food supply necessarily meant that some people would go hungry, an adequate overall food supply did not, in itself, guarantee that all people would have access to food sufficient for an active, healthy life. Thus, the theory of entitlements to food, and particularly entitlement failures of certain groups of people, has justifiably dominated food security analysis for much of the past two decades. Yet food aid as a key instrument used to address problems of hunger and food security still tends to be based on the assumption that the lack of food itself is the problem.[1]

To paraphrase this passage, change its structure by starting at a place other than the beginning, depending on the focus of your policy story. If you do, you'll naturally change some wording. For example, you could start with the second-to-last sentence, which discusses the theory of entitlements to food. Or you could focus on the people being written about. Focusing on people rather than abstractions (e.g., theoretical and empirical advances) will make your paraphrase more readable. You could also consider breaking up long sentences, combining shorter ones, or expanding on certain points to improve clarity. Doing so will help you eliminate some words and change others.

Here's one of the many ways you could paraphrase (and quote from) the passage above by changing its structure and focusing on the people:

> In the 1970s and 1980s, food aid programs were persuaded by researchers who argued that a lack of food was the main reason people went hungry. As a result, food aid programs focused on distributing as much food aid as possible. This "theory of entitlements to food," however, does not account for other issues that could be contributing to food insecurity. According to Christopher B. Barrett and Daniel G. Maxwell, authors of *Food Aid after Fifty Years,* the reality is that "while an inadequate overall food supply necessarily meant that some people would go hungry, an adequate overall food supply did not, in itself, guarantee that all people would have access to food sufficient for an active, healthy life."[2]

The key here is to avoid duplicating the author's expression and sentence structure. If you cite the source material as I did by inserting note 2 at the end of paragraph, you should have no worries about unintentionally plagiarizing another person's words and ideas.

One thing to remember: In policy writing—as is true in all academic and professional disciplines—some terminology is so specialized or conventional that it's impossible to paraphrase it without using wordy or awkward alternatives that will be less familiar to your readers. When you use such terminology, you are *not* stealing the unique phrasing of an individual writer. You are using a common vocabulary shared by members of a discipline or profession.

That's all I've got for you in terms of quoting and paraphrasing sources properly. In the next chapter, my friend and colleague James Bennett shows you how to use a variety of visuals to tell policy stories that matter. James is a self-described "recovering journalist" who spent two award-winning decades bringing his visual firepower to bear for publications on both coasts of the United States and many places in between—including stints as a news artist at the *Orange County*

Register and as a graphics editor at the venerable *Boston Globe*. Before fleeing daily journalism for the glamor and excitement of federal employment, James had become the assistant managing editor at the *Bakersfield Californian*. Now he helps Congress make better-informed decisions as a visual communication analyst for the Government Accountability Office. In short, he's darned good at what he does.

CHAPTER 13

Making Figures, Tables, and Charts Work for You

James Bennett

Communicating without visuals leaves you with one powerful hand tied behind your back. Before we take a closer look at visuals in public policy writing that matters, let's consider the following:

- The presence of a visual element makes anything much more likely to be noticed, read, and shared on social media.
- Adding visuals to a message increases the likelihood that a reader's perception of an issue will be influenced. Advertisers trade on the power of visuals.
- Many academic studies have shown that presenting information visually makes it dramatically easier for readers to understand and remember what they've read.
- Scientists estimate that a sizable portion of our brains—perhaps as much as one-third—is devoted to processing visual information. That's a lot of real estate considering all the other things your brain must do.

With the proliferation of infographics and other visuals on the internet, it's hardly surprising that many people think graphics are a modern phenomenon. In truth, graphics have been around as long as humans have. Even the letters that form the words you're reading right now can be traced to the drawings of our ancestors. When you think about it, the rising popularity of graphics is just a return to our roots in order to make sense of an increasingly complicated modern world.

WHAT IS A GRAPHIC?

For a discipline with ancient traditions, visual communication has a shockingly inconsistent vocabulary. Partly because every graphic is a custom act of communication, you'll find as many definitions for the term *graphic* as there are people who create them. While Shakespeare's "A rose by any other name would smell as sweet" argument is well taken, it is always helpful when we can agree on some key terms. Practically speaking, *graphics* are an organized combination of words and images that together convey meaning and/or explain something better than either could do alone.

Although the information age has spawned a few new terms for visual communication—like *data visualization* and *infographic*—we shouldn't be dazzled by jargon. Trendy "innovations" in graphics are more about format than meaningful differences. In the end, they're all just different ways of organizing and combining words and images.

There are many kinds of graphics, including charts, maps, and diagrams.

- *Charts* use math to translate numeric data into a visual form. There are many types of charts, but each type reveals the differences in a data set.
- *Maps* show geographic relationships and put places and distances into context, which can be critical to your reader's understanding. It's no accident that J. R. R. Tolkien put a map of Middle-earth on the opening pages of *The Hobbit*. He knew readers would struggle to keep all its places straight without a map to refer to.
- *Diagrams* are like maps of an object or a system. They show the parts in the context of the whole, the members in relation in a network, or how a system or process works. Diagrams are better than photos at explaining how something works because the designer can remove all the unimportant details, allowing readers to focus on the point of the graphic.

- *Infographics* used to be a term for any moderately complicated visual created for a print publication. Most people now use it to describe a collection of related visual elements organized in a vertical, "scrollable" format, which makes it ideal for viewing on a computer screen. If well done, infographics can give an overview of a subject that may have otherwise required an extensive amount of text to explain.
- *Data visualization* is a relatively new term for any complex depiction of a large data set. Data visualizations work better online, where users can interact with portions of the data while still seeing how each bit of information fits into a larger whole. In print, we sometimes make them with several charts working in concert. Data visualizations are like people: they're all beautiful in their own way, but not all of them have something interesting to say.

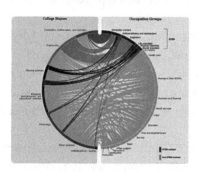

A brief note about text in graphics: The balance of words and images is a test of the effectiveness of a graphic. Some text is vital to letting readers know what the visuals show, but a lot of text is a sign that the visuals aren't doing enough work. For the best results, limit text to describing things the visuals cannot represent, such as units of measure (i.e., "millions of dollars") or a proper name. Try to devote no more than 20 percent of a graphic's total space to text.

THE VISUAL TOOLBOX

Experienced visual communicators treat the range of graphics like the tools in a well-stocked toolbox. Things get done because visual communicators value each tool for what it does, and they take the time to match each tool to the presentation of a particular type of information. Inexperienced visual communicators pick the tool before fully considering the job, which is a recipe for failure. It's not enough to know that we need to dig. The size of the required hole should dictate whether we get out the garden trowel or the backhoe.

Because equipping even a simple toolbox for visual communication can feel overwhelming, let's start with something simple—the questioning model that new journalists are taught. Reporters know they're ready to write when they have answers to six classic questions: Who? What? When? Where? Why? How? Knowing which of those questions you're trying to answer with your graphic will help suggest the graphic that will show it best. Once you've mastered the basic tools, you can modify and combine them as needed to create whatever will show your message best.

Who graphics are called for when relationships are an important part of your story. In the public policy arena, the "who" is usually an organization, not an individual.

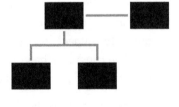

Organizational charts show the members of an organization and their relationship to one another in a hierarchical arrangement where entities (people, offices, etc.) are set above the entities they oversee with lines connecting them.

What graphics are called for when you have lots of numbers or important trends to show. They're often signaled in the text by verbs such as *rose, fell,* or *remained.* "What" questions are best answered by showing the data underlying the trend in question, and nothing does that like a chart.

Charts are all about converting numbers into a visual form, but no two types of chart represent their numbers in the same way. More on charts later.

Photos are a great tool for documenting current conditions because they capture *what* was happening at a point in time. Moreover, photos capture a tremendous amount of information, and they can be incredibly persuasive or emotional. Before you decide to include photos in your report, consult your organization's rules so that your photos conform. For example, federal agencies in the United States prefer not to show faces of people in photos.

When graphics make most people think of timelines, but that's not always the best way to convey important dates to your readers.

Timelines are really a chart of how much time elapsed between events. If the time between events isn't important, don't foist a timeline on your readers. The lines required to connect an event and its description to the right point on a timeline can make the graphic hard to read. If you do need a timeline, keep each entry as short as possible. Five words or fewer is best.

Railroads | **Space shuttle**

1900 1920 1940 1960 1980 2000

Chronology, on the other hand, is the fancy name for a simple list of key events in order by date. Be sure to refer to it as a "chronology" instead of saying "a list of events." That consoles anybody who's disappointed they're not getting a timeline. If they're still upset, you might point out that nobody *needs* a timeline to know that 1945 happened after 1920. A simple list of key dates is all most projects need.

Where graphics are all about boundaries, geographic relationships, and scale. Most of the time, showing anything like that requires a map.

Maps show physical relationships, and they locate places in relation to one another. Having a scale on a map is usually necessary so that readers can judge the distance between locations. Maps may be improved by adding "layers" of information, such as fire stations, areas zoned residential, or power lines—provided that the information adds to the message.

Choropleth maps assign to each geographic area (e.g., state or county) a color that varies in relation to a range of values in an underlying data set. Frequently the darkest color signifies the top of the range. Be sure to convert your data to rates (e.g., number of college students per 10,000 residents) or percentages (e.g., percentage of college students who are working full-time) when creating choropleth maps. If you use raw numbers, you'll tend to "light up" areas with bigger populations because there is more activity of all kinds (veterans, skate parks, home loans) where there are more people.

Data maps combine "where" with "what" by displaying a chart element and linking it to a specific location. For example, a data map could locate every Department of Veterans Affairs hospital and then put on top of that location a circle scaled to the number of military veterans who used the facility in the past year.

Why graphics are nearly impossible to do well because "why" is a nearly impossible question for graphics to answer. Nine times out of 10, you're better off not even trying. Instead, make sure you're answering "why" in the text. Getting information isn't the problem in the internet age. The real problem is that few people have the time to sort it or explain what it means. That means readers are counting on your insights into the cause(s) of a problem or challenge. Devote as much text as possible to explaining "why" a problem is occurring; that will help inspire your readers to become engaged.

How graphics can be quite effective because "how" is the best question to answer with a graphic. Anytime you face "how it works" or "how it happened" questions, a graphic will do a magnificent job of telling the story. The same details that can make a paragraph confusing are the building blocks for a graphic that *shows* readers how something works. Think of it this way: Ikea furniture is hard enough to assemble with just pictures. Imagine trying to turn that pile of lumber into a bookcase with only text to guide you. That's what you're asking readers to do when you try to answer "how" questions without a graphic.

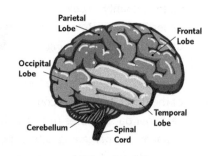

Diagrams show the parts of something and reveal how those parts work together to achieve a particular outcome. These visual depictions of physical relationships can be thought of as a kind of map of a thing or a process. This is a step up from a glossary because individual components are also "defined" by what they look like and how they fit with the other parts. But don't get overly excited about the details: diagrams are best when you downplay, or even exclude, unimportant components.

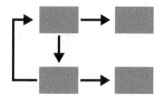

Flowcharts display the key steps in a process and what happens at critical decision points. For example, the benefits enrollment process for Veterans Affairs continues to the next step, when a veteran's application is complete, but it also branches off in another direction when an incomplete application requires that staff gather additional documentation. The conditional information in a flowchart invites readers to "play along" with a process and allows a static print graphic to seem a little like an interactive graphic on the internet.

SETTING THE TABLE FOR AN EFFECTIVE CHART

As we discussed earlier, charts convert numeric data into a visual form, allowing readers to see trends and make comparisons. No charting can begin, however, until you organize the data into the rows (horizontal) and columns (vertical) of a table. Putting data into a table also points out missing data and any trends or outliers that deserve further research.

Tables and charts are both viable vehicles for information, but tables will never match the visual horsepower of charts because most readers won't bother with the tedious task of comparing the individual data points. Still, while tables will never be "sexy," they do have three major strengths.

First, tables allow readers to compare lots of unlike values. The last time you made a major purchase you may have consulted a table to compare the key features of similar products or services. Tables work well because disparate measurements (e.g., price, weight, size, power, or time) can happily live side by side in a table. Mixing those unlike values would quickly turn a chart into an unreadable jumble.

Second, tables convey precise values. If the numbers you want readers to see are very close in value, and those minor differences are important, you're probably better off with a table than a chart. In most cases, readers can't see the differences in chart elements representing nearly identical values.

Third, tables can save pages of text. By eliminating many of the words necessary to relate in prose what data a table contains, you'll save yourself space. Plus, readers can easily find the important categories (because they're row or column labels), and none of those categories must be repeated for readers to make a comparison.

A QUICK LOOK AT CHARTS

Charts use math to translate numeric data into a visual form. This allows a reader's brain to see a pattern it can understand and remember. Many books have been written on how to do this effectively, so we'll stick with the basics. There are many types of charts, as shown in table 13.1, but most of them work by varying *one* visual factor (e.g., length, width, height, or area) per data point in an underlying data set.

TABLE 13.1. Types of charts

Name	Best for
Bar (a.k.a. column)	Bar charts show one-time (e.g., daily or monthly) measurements across categories or over time. Bar charts are just as effective when oriented horizontally (with bars pointing to the right) as they are vertically.
Stacked bar	This format turns each bar into a mini pie chart. If each bar represents a different year or other unit of time, using a stacked bar will show readers how the components in each bar change over time. For best results, follow the rules for pie charts.
Cluster bar	Cluster bars "unstack" the data to let readers compare the components directly (e.g., a set of bars from 1990 to 2000 for the US Army, Navy, Air Force, and Marines). The message of cluster bars changes depending on their arrangement (e.g., a bar for the four armed services each year or all the Army bars followed by all the Navy bars, etc.).
Range (a.k.a. hi-lo or box-and-whisker)	Range charts work like bars, but they add "tails" that show the lowest and highest measurement in the category each bar represents. Statisticians love the detail and accuracy of these charts, but they call a lot of attention to the outliers in each category, which may not be desirable in some cases.
Line (a.k.a. fever)	Line charts compare constant measurements across categories or over time. They emphasize the trend because individual data points are hard to see on the line.
Pie	Pie charts divide a circle into slices that represent the data proportionally. It can be hard for readers to discern minor differences in the slices, so these charts work best for unequal divisions. Try to limit the number of slices in your pie to five or fewer.

TABLE 13.1. (cont.)

Name	Best for
"Zoom" pie	When readers need to see how one slice breaks down into further slices, add a second pie chart that "zooms" out of its parent. This reveals the "X percent of Y percent" type of detail that is otherwise hard to understand. These "sub-pies" should be kept to scale (i.e., be smaller) relative to the original pie.
Area (a.k.a. mountain)	If a line chart and a pie chart had a baby, it would be an area chart. These cool charts show the shift in each component's share over time. They're especially good at showing the "wave" when one category grows from a minor to a major factor.
Scatter (a.k.a. scatter plot)	Scatter charts or plots are the only safe way to show "apples and oranges" data in the same chart. They work by putting one related but unlike data set on the y-axis, with the other on the x-axis, and marking their intersection with a small icon (usually a box or circle). A scatter chart with grade point average on the y-axis and totals of students' loans on the x-axis would mark the cost of each student's achievement.

HOW TO TELL WHEN YOU NEED A GRAPHIC

If we tried hard enough, we could come up with a graphic for *every* element in a public policy report. We'd have lots of visuals, but only a few of them would add anything to our message. Having too many graphics is nearly as daunting to readers as too much text. Ask yourself, "What would a graphic show?" and save your attempts at visuals for the classic reporter questions (five *W*s and an *H*) that graphics answer best. At the same time, a graphic may be the solution *whenever you are . . .*

- *struggling with a lot of numbers in the text*. Even a relatively simple comparison gets confusing when multiple years and lots of numbers are involved. Replace that convoluted sentence with a chart.

- *wanting readers to remember recurring or important information.* The type of information tells you what kind of graphic you need. Places need a map; "nouns" need a diagram; dates need a chronology or timeline; processes need a flowchart; and so on.
- *having trouble explaining how something works.* Remember the Ikea furniture analogy, and don't risk losing readers by attempting to describe a complicated process with words alone. Show them with a diagram how the process works, and tell them in the text why they should care. Making a drawing of a process is also a great way to check and refine your own understanding of it. Start with a rough sketch, and don't worry about making it pretty until you are sure readers need more details.

FIVE WAYS TO MAKE ANY GRAPHIC BETTER

First, and above all else, work with convention. Cliché isn't a bad thing with visuals. Icons bear the "classic" representation of an item for a reason. Nobody may attend a little red schoolhouse anymore, but we still show the steeple and bell in a school icon. Remember the same principle when using color: don't use red to represent cold or put tan water around blue land on a map. Likewise, readers of English will expect to find information in order from top to bottom and left to right. A process should flow from the first step at the left (or top) to the last at the right (or bottom). The same goes for time in a chart, chronology, or timeline. Start with the oldest date at the left (or top) and move to the newest at the right (or bottom). Remember that anything you do to defy convention will make it harder for readers to take in the information of your graphic quickly.

Second, make differences mean something. Readers are easily distracted by even minor variations in a visual presentation. They will notice the 12 colors you gave the bars in a chart to make it "pretty" as much or more than they will notice the differences in the heights of those bars. But only one of those differences is important. Make sure any variation helps reveal your message by keeping everything else as simple and consistent as possible. The visual representation of anything (e.g., chart elements measuring veterans or icons showing college graduates) should remain visually consistent throughout a report.

Third, draw the verb. Make sure there is a visual representation of any important action you're describing in the text. A diagram about how veterans access health services should show how a veteran gets admitted to a Veterans Affairs facility. A chart next to a paragraph about an increase in wait times should show the bars or lines rising, too.

Fourth, adopt a visual style and stick to it. Especially when more than one person is creating graphics, it's always better to agree ahead of time on a general look for your visuals and to share those expectations with everyone. This saves your graphic creators the time of dreaming up a novel way of showing things and makes it more likely the finished report will look like a coherent whole. Moreover, use visual clues to group information. Differences in size, style (bold, italic, etc.), and color of type help guide readers to what you want them to see. Less important information, such as axis labels, should be smaller and less conspicuous than more important information, such as value labels. Color should always be used to communicate, not to decorate. Making all the water labels blue or all the veteran chart elements green helps readers group like information. Color choices should be logical, and each color should be given only one "job" per graphic. (E.g., green should not show veteran data *and* federal spending.)

Last, keep the "furniture" to a minimum. Inexperienced visual communicators often give too much emphasis to grid lines and other less important elements in charts and diagrams. Fade back or remove things like grid lines so that readers can focus on the information instead of its container. Directly labeling is always better than forcing readers to decode the meaning of chart or map elements by referring to a legend.

CHAPTER 14

A Style Guide for Policy Writing

When I started working at the Harris School of Public Policy, one of the first things I did was put together this style guide to help students write correctly, consistently, and clearly. It provides guidance on those style issues—including capitalization, punctuation, and word usage—most relevant to public policy.

Have you ever wondered or worried, for example, about what was correct:

- Periods or punctuation for bulleted lists?
- "Which" or "that"?
- % or "percent"?

If so, you're in luck. What follows provides quick answers to these sorts of questions.

Consistently following a style guide like this one will help give your writing a uniformity that conveys professionalism. Inconsistencies in style or misused words can cause readers to question the accuracy of your data, analysis, and conclusions. Nobody wants that.

Are what follow hard-and-fast rules? No. This is a style guide—not a rule book. Many of the "writing rules" we grew up memorizing are not really rules as much as they are preferences perpetuated by grammarians, teachers, and editors. If you have a question that isn't covered in this guide, or if there is a topic you'd like to know more about, here are three online references that are worth consulting:

- *Chicago Manual of Style*
- *U.S. Government Printing Office Style Manual*
- *Merriam-Webster's Collegiate Dictionary*

ABBREVIATIONS

- General Rules
  - Use as few abbreviations as possible.
  - Do not use an abbreviation before it has been introduced parenthetically.
    - To introduce an abbreviation, spell out the term you want to abbreviate, and follow it with its abbreviation in parentheses.
      - *Example*: Department of Education (Education)
  - Reintroduce abbreviations in report appendixes. Because of the brevity of most appendixes, it is customary to reintroduce abbreviations only once for all appendixes.
  - Consider including a list of abbreviations, and what they stand for, in longer policy reports.
- Punctuation
  - Omit periods and spaces in the acronyms of government agencies, programs, and other organizations (e.g., GAO, DOD, and FDIC).
  - Omit periods in "Washington, DC."
  - Use periods when abbreviating units of time, measurement, and first and middle names.
    - *Examples*: a.m., lbs., and J. M. Jones (note the space between the first and middle initials).
- Organizations and Programs
  - In titles, headings, and executive summaries, use only familiar acronyms such as IRS and NASA.
  - To make an abbreviation plural, add "s" (e.g., HMOs).
  - Form possessives as you would with a word (e.g., DOD's status, the HMO's representative). If the last letter of an abbreviation is "s," form the possessive by adding an apostrophe and "s" (e.g., HHS's regulations, not HHS' regulations).
  - Do not use "the" before an abbreviation (e.g., according to DOD, not according to the DOD).
    - *Exceptions*: abbreviations used as adjectives (e.g., the FAA data) and abbreviations that are generally preceded by "the" in common usage (e.g., the FBI).

- Geographic Terms
  - Spell out "United States" whenever it is used as a noun (e.g., laws of the United States). Use "US" only as an adjective (e.g., US law).
  - Spell out the names of states and territories in text.
  - May use postal abbreviations in tables and figures (e.g., CA or FL).
- Latin Abbreviations
  - Latin abbreviations may be used in parenthetical expressions, but in text, use English terms:
    - "that is" instead of "i.e."
    - "for example" instead of "e.g."
    - "and so forth" instead of "etc."
- People's Names and Titles
  - Spell out civil and military titles preceding a full name or a surname alone.
    - Senator A. B. Smith; Senator Smith
    - Chief Justice John Marshall; Chief Justice Marshall
    - Secretary of State John Foster Dulles; Secretary Dulles
    - Rear Admiral Jane Doe; Rear Admiral Doe
- Miscellaneous
  - Write out "fiscal year" in text; "FY" may be used in figures and tables as long as the abbreviation is defined in a footnote or legend.
  - Do not abbreviate "miles per hour" in text.
  - In contexts where dollar-based currencies need to be identified, do not use periods: US$20, C$30 or Can$30, NZ$40, A$50. Also: 3 million British pounds or £3 million; 150 euros or €150
  - Spell out "company" and "corporation" if they are part of a company's name (e.g., XYZ Corporation).

ARTICLES

Articles (a, an, the) precede nouns. Choosing the right one can be pretty tricky because article usage depends on the noun itself and its meaning in the sentence. There is a six-step method to for choosing the appropriate article.

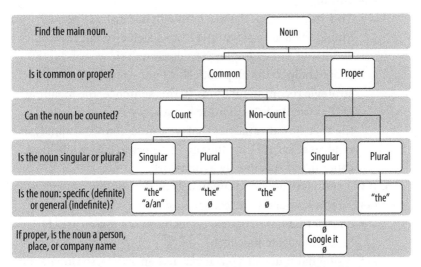

Decision tree for choosing the appropriate article. Source: Adapted from Marianne Celce-Murcia and Diane Larsen-Freeman, *The Grammar Book: An ESL/ELL Teacher's Course*, 2nd ed. (Boston: Heinle and Heinle, 1999)

1. Find the noun.
   - A noun is a word used to identify a person, place, or thing (common noun) or to name a one of these (proper noun).
2. Is the noun in this instance common or proper?
   - Common nouns are everyday nouns (e.g., data, memo, program).
   - Proper nouns start with a capital letter and are names or titles (e.g., President Obama, Microsoft, US Congress).
3. Is the noun countable?
   - A countable noun names something that can exist in a discrete, individual unit and be made plural (e.g., officials, laws, landowners).
   - A non-count noun is thought of as a whole and cannot be broken into parts (e.g., education, weather, information).

4. Is the noun singular or plural?
   - Pay attention to collective nouns (like committee) as some collective nouns, depending on context, can be considered either plural or singular.
5. Determine if the noun's meaning is specific (definite) or general (indefinite).
   - This step is one of the most difficult because the noun's intended meaning should dictate specificity, not the noun's definition. For example: "The data analysis we conducted should help us develop both short-term and long-term strategic recommendations In this sentence, the meaning of "data analysis" is definite because we are talking about the specific data analysis that we conducted. "Data analysis is never easy," on the other hand, refers to data analysis in general, not specifically to our work.
6. If the noun is proper and singular, then decide what the name denotes. Is it a person, place, or company?
   - Singular names of people typically do not use an article (e.g., Dean Kate Baicker).
   - A singular name of a place may use an article, so Google the name to check (e.g., the Willis tower, Merchandise Mart).
   - Singular company or institutional names usually do not require articles (e.g., Apple, Google), though sometimes they do (e.g., the University of Chicago, the Harris School of Public Policy).

LISTS

Some bulleted lists are introduced by a phrase, and the items in the list are also phrases:

- The introductory phrase and the bulleted items together must read as a complete sentence.
- Lowercase the items and separate them with commas (or semicolons if at least one of the phrases has internal commas).
- Insert "and" or "or" after the penultimate item and place a period after the last item.

- *Example*: The agency could
  - cancel the agreement immediately,
  - extend the agreement past its expiration, or
  - develop a new agreement.

Other bulleted lists are introduced by a complete sentence, and the items are either all phrases or complete sentences. For both kinds, end the sentence introducing the list with a colon.

When the listed items are phrases:

- If the list is composed of phrases, lowercase the phrases and separate them using commas (or semicolons if at least one phrase has internal commas).
- Insert "and" or "or" after the penultimate item and a period after the last item.
- *Example*: Possible actions include the following:
  - maintaining the status quo;
  - amending the scope, methodology, and strategy; or
  - devising a new approach.

When the listed items are complete sentences:

- If the list is composed of complete sentences, treat each sentence as you would in regular text by capitalizing the first word and place a period or question mark at the end.
- *Example*: Possible actions include the following:
  - The bureau could reevaluate its strategy.
  - The task force could devise a new approach.
  - The director could reconfigure the work group.

When the listed items are fronted by numbers instead of bullets, keep in mind the following points:

- If numbered items are used, a period follows the numeral.
- All items—even phrases—begin with a capital letter.
- *Example*: Use three performance measures:
  1. Percentage of the US population.

2. Number of communities taking actions.

3. Potential property losses, disaster, and other costs.

Here are some tips for creating lists:

- With lengthy bulleted items covering a range of topics, consider beginning each item with a topic heading (i.e., a word or brief phrase, set off in italics or bolded type) that helps readers quickly identify the topic.
- Maintain parallel construction for each item in a list. For example, use all gerunds, commands, nouns, or complete sentences for each item in the list. Do not mix and match.

CAPITALIZATION

- General Guidance
  - Capitalize the full and shortened names of administrative, deliberative, judicial, and legislative bodies, as well as departments, bureaus, and offices.
    - Bureau of the Census; Census Bureau
    - Department of State; State Department
    - United Nations Security Council; the Security Council
    - House of Representatives; the House
  - Use lowercase nouns when used in place of the names of governmental bodies.
    - agency
    - committee
    - department
    - office
  - Use lowercase "federal," "state," "act," and other shortened forms of official names.
    - the federal government
    - the act passed in 1996
    - the food program
  - Use lowercase for "presidential" and "administration."
  - Capitalize people's titles when the title precedes their name.

- Assistant Director Jane Does
- Vice President Joe Biden
  - Use lowercase when a title is part of a descriptive phrase or preceded by "the."
    - former president Kennedy
    - the then secretary of state George Shultz
  - Use lowercase titles when they follow someone's name (an appositive) or appear in isolation.
    - Xi Jinping, president of China
    - the secretary of state
    - members of Congress
    - the chief justice of the United States
    - the director
  - Capitalize the first word after a colon when it begins a question or when a colon introduces two or more sentences.
    - The study's findings focused on a single issue: Should the agency be restructured?
  - Items in a bulleted list begin with capital letters only if each item is a complete sentence that ends with a period.
- Titles and Headings
  - Lowercase "to" even when used with an infinitive.
  - Lowercase articles (i.e., "a" and "the"), prepositions (even long ones such as "through" and "between"), and coordinating conjunctions (e.g., and, or, but, for, so, nor, yet).
  - Capitalize all adjectives, adverbs, nouns, pronouns, subordinating conjunctions (e.g., although, because, that, where, whether, therefore), and verbs.
  - Capitalize the words following a hyphen, except when what comes in front of the hyphen is a prefix that cannot stand alone as a word.
    - Only the first letter in "Anti-intellectual" and "E-commerce" should be capitalized.
    - Both "One" and "Third" would be capitalized in "One-Third of the Agencies Agreed"
- Regional Terms
  - Regional terms are generally capitalized (e.g., Northwest, South, and East), but adjectives and nouns derived from

those terms are usually lowercase (e.g., northwesterner). Other examples:

- central New York
- the Continent (Europe) but the continental United States
- Great Plains, northern plains, plains
- Northern California, Southern California
- New York State, Washington State
- West Coast, East Coast
- western states, Western world

NUMBERS

- General Guidance
  - Spell out zero through nine.
  - In general, use numbers for 10 and higher.
  - Ordinals follow the same general rule as numbers.
    - words for "first" through "ninth"
    - numerals for "10th" and higher (usually)
- Exceptions
  - Spell out any number that begins a sentence, and try to revise awkward sentences by preceding the number with a word.
    - "Twenty-four hours later . . ."
    - "The year 2020 brought many changes."
  - Use numerals for all common elements in a series if any element includes a number that is 10 or higher. Treat numbers consistently within the same context (i.e., sentence, paragraph, or section).
    - An average of **32 children** in five schools lived in two different counties. Of these children, **5** did not live near a bus route.
  - Use numerals for parts of a publication:
    - figure 7, table 4
    - footnote 3, volume 6
    - page 2, section 9
  - Use may use numerals before units of measure (area, distance, length, mass, percentages, pressure, temperature,

time, and volume). It is also acceptable to use numerals for
for time and ages—no matter how small.

- o Other examples

2 years old, a 1-year-old	3 hours 2 minutes
a 3-year-old treaty	10:00 a.m.
4 miles, second mile	6 months, 2 years
8-mile radius, 7 acres	3 fiscal years
5-foot-wide entrance	the 1990s
3 feet 5-1/4 inches tall	30-day period
80 cents, $12.50, $100	four decades
$1 million	in any one year
1 percent, 0.2 percent	5 degrees Celsius
4 gallons, 30 psi	6 watts, 8 volts

- Fractions
  - o Follow the same general rule as with numbers.
    - ▪ Use numerals for 1/10 and smaller fractions (e.g., 3/20 of an inch), but spell out larger fractions (e.g., one-half, three-quarters).
  - o Spelled-out fractions are hyphenated both as nouns and adjectives:
    - ▪ two-thirds of the class
    - ▪ a two-thirds majority
    - ▪ Use numerals for any number that includes a decimal and place a zero before decimal fractions smaller than one (e.g., 1.3 and 0.02).
  - o Use the same measure throughout a passage. For example, do not use "one-quarter of the children and 50 percent of the adults."
- Punctuation
  - o When a month and date appear before a year, the year is preceded and followed by a comma, but when no date appears between the month and year, no comma in needed.
    - ▪ The January 12, 2011, letter said that . . .
    - ▪ The January 2011 letter said that . . .
  - o When a number is the first element of a modifier, hyphenate the compound:
    - ▪ 7-inch square
    - ▪ four-engine plane

- Dollar figures and percentages are not hyphenated when used as modifiers:
  - the $5 million request
  - a 5 percent increase
- Hyphenate numbers appearing before the word "ratio":
  - a 10-to-1 ration
  - a ratio of 10 to 1
- Place a space after the first hyphen in a dimension used as a modifier:
  - an 11- by 17-inch sheet of paper
- Omit the apostrophe when writing decades (e.g., 1990s).
- Other examples:
  - 1 month's pay
  - 2-1/2 times
  - 2 hours' work
  - 40-plus people
  - uranium-235

- Ranges
  - When "from" precedes the first item in a range, follow it with "to" or "through," as appropriate.
    - Negotiations were held from 2002 to 2010 [i.e., for at least part of 2002 and 2010].
    - Negotiations were held from March 15 through June.
  - When "between" precedes the first item in a range, separate the items with "and."
    - The meeting was held between noon and 4 p.m. *Note*: "Between" indicates an interval (e.g., of time or space) or separation. It is often not the clearest choice when expressing a range of years; instead, "from . . . to/through" is more precise.

PUNCTUATION

Apostrophe

- General Guidance
  - Form the possessive of most singular words and acronyms by adding an apostrophe and "s."

- witness's
- HHS's
- Arkansas's
- Director Burns's
- secretary-treasurer's
- *Exception*: Marine Corps'

o Form the possessive of almost all plural nouns by adding an apostrophe only.
  - the presidents'
  - First and Sixth Divisions'
  - the taxpayers'

- Joint versus separate possession
  o If elements in a series are considered a single unit or encompass joint "ownership," the possessive falls on the last element.
    - Minneapolis and St. Paul's transportation system
  o If the elements' ownership is separate, make each element possessive.
    - New York's and Chicago's transportation systems
- When *not* to use an apostrophe
  o Do not use an apostrophe to form
    - the plural of spelled-out numbers (e.g., twos and threes) or
    - the plural of acronyms (e.g., five HMOs).

Brackets

- Bracket any clarifying words you add to a quotation.
  o "Despite [the panel's] report, the agency still supports the program."

Colon

- Use a colon to introduce statements, questions, or explanatory material. If a question follows a colon, begin the sentence with a capital letter. When an incomplete sentence follows a colon, lowercase the first word unless it normally would be capitalized.
  o Only one question was discussed: What policy should be adopted?

- ○ The board consists of three officials: a chair, vice chair, and a recorder.
- Use a colon to introduce a bulleted list. The introductory statement must be a complete sentence.
  - ○ We recommend that the commissioner of the IRS do the following things:
    - ▪ Evaluate the act's provisions.
    - ▪ Monitor taxpayer compliance.
    - ▪ Inform Congress of actions taken.

Comma

- Use commas to separate three or more items in a series, including the last word before "and." However, if a series contains internal punctuation, separate the major items with a semicolon.
  - ○ The report went to the senator, EPA, and state committees.
  - ○ Unsafe conditions included leaking oil; deteriorated, damaged, or missing railings; and improperly stored chemicals.
- Set off introductory phrases, parenthetical expressions, and dependent clauses with a comma.
  - ○ According to the officials, the agency has certified few inspectors.
  - ○ The database, the secretary reported, will be validated by June.
  - ○ After the hard drive crashed, the data were retrieved from the file server.
- If a subject has two predicates, a comma is usually not needed between the predicates.
  - ○ FAA has few inspectors but plans to roll out a new training program.
- Enclose a state with commas when it follows a city. *Note*: The state may be omitted for major cities.
  - ○ The task force inspected the Rockville, Maryland, branch but not the Boston headquarters.
- When an exclamation point or a question mark appears at the end of a quotation where a comma would typically appear, omit the comma.
  - ○ "Why is the program ineffective?" the official asked.

- The title of a work that ends in an exclamation point or a question mark should be followed by a comma if the grammar of the sentence would typically call for one.
  - The Beatle's most popular albums—*A Hard Day's Night, Help!*, and *Yellow Submarine*—continue to sell well.

Dash

- Use *em dashes* to indicate sudden changes in tone, a thought interrupting a sentence, or to set off a series.
  - To emphasize a contradiction between ideas:
    - He said—no one contradicted him—that the battle was lost.
  - To insert parenthetical commentary while emphasizing its importance (parentheses tend to diminish the importance of what's enclosed in them):
    - We visited the three DOE sites—Hanford, Savannah, and Idaho National Laboratory—that store spent nuclear fuel.
  - To connect ideas to each other:
    - To feed, clothe, and find shelter for the needy—these are real achievements.

Ellipsis

- An ellipsis is used to indicate an omission in quoted material.
- Technical matters:
  - Place a space between all ellipsis periods.
  - In a three-period ellipsis—indicating material has been omitted from the middle of a sentence—also place a space on either side of the end periods.
  - When the last part of a quoted sentence is omitted, use four periods.
  - Ellipsis periods are not used before the first word of a partial quotation.
  - When formatted, ellipsis periods should always appear on the same line.

- Examples:
  - ○ "DOD officials denied the investigators access . . . for several reasons."
  - ○ "DOD officials denied the investigators access. . . . Later, after videotapes were released, the officials apologized."
  - ○ DOD officials said the videotapes "did not include footage from the participants' discussion."

Exclamation Point

- Generally avoid using the exclamation point unless you are quoting material that contains one.

Parentheses

- Use parentheses to set off expressions from surrounding material. Note the placement of the period in the following examples.
  - ○ The increase amounted to $2.5 billion over 5 years (as shown in table 4).
  - ○ The increase amounted to $2.5 billion over 5 years. (Table 4 shows the program's annual expenditures.)
- Use a pair of parentheses to enclose numerals designating items in a list.
  - ○ The task force (1) approved the work plan, (2) began collecting data, and (3) organized committees to validate the data.

Period

- Do not use periods with acronyms (generally). Abbreviations with uppercase and lowercase letters require them:
  - ○ Lt. Gen.
  - ○ Brig. Gen.
  - ○ Dr.
  - ○ Ms.
  - ○ Jr.
  - ○ Pub. K. No.
- For people's initials, place a space after each period (e.g., I. M. Johnson).

Quotation Marks

- Do not use quotation marks to enclose any matter preceded by "so-called."
  - The workers' attendance was recorded in the so-called captain's log.
- Place punctuation inside or outside quotation marks as follows:
  - Commas and periods go inside closing quotation marks.
  - Colons and semicolons follow closing quotation marks.
  - Other punctuation marks are placed inside quotation marks only if they are a part of the quoted matter.
    - We asked, "What are the program's biggest challenges?" *But*: Why call it a "gentlemen's agreement"?

Quotations

- A long quotation running multiple lines is indented from the left margin and a line space is placed above and below the quoted text. A quotation set off this way is not enclosed in quotation marks. To show author-added emphasis, such as italics, use brackets.
  - Postal Service officials made the following comment:
    When we build or leave new facilities, we install the appropriate level of security technology, such as *electronic access controls* and *closed-circuit camera systems* [emphasis added], based on the requirement specified in our physical security regulations.
- For quotes that include more than one paragraph, indent the first line of the second paragraph and any others.
  - Postal Service officials made the following comment:
    When we build or lease new facilities, we install the appropriate level of security technology, such as electronic access controls and closed-circuit camera systems, based on the mandatory requirements specified in our physical security regulations.

    For existing facilities, we work with local managers to prioritize their security needs and develop cost-effective solutions to increase compliance with security requirements.

Semicolon

- Use a semicolon to join two thoughts that could otherwise stand as separate sentences but that are closely linked.
  - The computer engineering firm violated SBA's regulations; for example, it did not inform SBA of the true equity ownership in the firm.
- Use a semicolon to separate three or more phrases or clauses with internal punctuation.
  - If you want your writing to be worthwhile, give it unity; if you want it to be easy to read, give it coherence; and if you want it to be interesting, give it emphasis.
- Do not use semicolons to separate numbered items that contain no internal punctuation.
  - Information can be arranged by (1) time sequence, (2) order of importance, or (3) subject classification.
- Use a semicolon to separate closely related statements.
  - War is destructive; peace, constructive.

SPELLING

Plurals irregular or unusual

- appendix; appendixes
- basis; bases
- criterion; criteria
- curriculum; curricula
- datum; data (e.g., "The data were correctly analyzed.")
- formula; formulas
- memorandum; memorandums
- minutia; minutiae
- money; moneys
- parenthesis; parentheses
- phenomenon; phenomena
- stimulus; stimuli
- synopsis; synopses

Compounds

- Prefixes
  - Nearly all compounds formed with the following prefixes are written as one word.
    - anti-, counter-, infra-, mid-, multi-, non-, over-, post-, pre-, re-, semi-, sub-, trans-, and under-
  - Some exceptions include
    - capitalized words or numerals (e.g., trans-Canada, mid-1998);
    - compounds containing more than one hyphenated word (e.g., non-interest-bearing bond); and
    - compounds with repeated vowels (e.g., anti-inflammatory).
- Commonly Used Compounds

African American	over-the-counter drugs
Chinese American	policy maker
cross section	policy making (n.)
cross-country	policy-making (adj.)
crosscutting	rule making (n.)
cost-effective	rule-making (adj.)
cost-effectiveness	self-determination
data-processing (adj.)	self-reported
decision maker	short-term CD
decision-making (n.)	sole-source procurement
decision-making (adj.)	soon-to-be-released
drawdown (n.)	staff member
draw down (v.)	tax-exempt investment
high-priority (adj.)	well-funded program
high-quality (adj.)	work flow
high-risk (adj.)	work hour
long-standing (adj.)	workday
long-term (adj.)	workforce
online (adj.)	workload
off-line (adj.)	workpapers
off-site (adj.)	workplace
on-site (adj.)	worksheet
out-of-date data	X-ray

- Compound Verbs
    - Write compound verbs ending in a preposition as two words. When they are used as nouns or adjectives, typically they are written as one word or hyphenated.
        - They were going to lay off 5,000 employees.
        - The layoff affected mostly corporate staff.

VERB	NOUN OR ADJECTIVE
back up	backup
break down	breakdown
build up	buildup
check up	checkup
follow up	follow-up
hand out	handout
run off	runoff
start up	start-up
trade off	trade-off

- Plural Forms
    - In forming plurals of compound terms that are hyphenated or written as two or more words, make the significant words plural.
    - Where the significant word is first:
        - ambassadors at large
        - attorneys at law
        - brothers-in-law
        - commanders in chief
        - courts-martial
        - notaries public
        - rights-of-way
    - Where the significant word is in the middle:
        - assistant attorneys general
        - assistant chiefs of staff
        - deputy chiefs of staff
    - Where the significant word is last:
        - assistant attorneys
        - assistant commissioners
        - assistant secretaries
        - deputy sheriffs

- o If no word is significant in itself, make the last word plural:
  - hand-me-downs
- Adjectival Compounds
  - o Compound adjectives that are hyphenated when they pre-cede a noun, as with color compounds, usually remain open when they follow the noun.

HYPHENATED	OPEN
emerald-green tie	The tie is emerald green
snow-white dress	The clouds are snow white
black-and-white print	The truth isn't black and white
XYZ is a well-managed agency	The agency is well managed

- Computer and Internet Terms

cyberspace	online
database	personal computer; PC
debug	random access memory
desktop	(RAM)
disk: hard disk, floppy disk	read-only memory (ROM)
download (n. and v.)	web
email (n. and v.)	webcast
handheld	web page
home page	website
hypertext	worksheet
internet; the net	workstation
intranet	World Wide Web
keystroke	write-only
laptop	write-protected
off-line	

VERBS

Subject-verb agreement is a rule of writing and speaking where the subject and verb of a sentence agree in number. A *singular subject* (Emily/she) takes a *singular verb* (is). A *plural subject* (they/we) uses a *plural verb* (are). Put simply: once you find the subject, make the verb agree.

Eight rules of subject-verb agreement

1. **Indefinite Pronouns**. Indefinite pronouns—everyone, each one, someone, somebody, no one, anyone, anybody, nobody—use a singular verb.

   *Everyone **is** happy about having fewer problems sets.*

2. **Here**, **There**. When starting a sentence using "here" or "there," the *subject* comes after the *verb*.

   *There **are** so many <u>assignments</u> this week.*
   *Here **is** the final <u>paper</u>.*

3. **Units of Measurement**. When discussing distances, periods of time, sums of money, etc. use a singular verb.

   *<u>26.2 miles</u> **is** the length of a marathon.*

   But when a percentage or a part of the whole is used, the verb becomes plural.

   *20 out of 100 <u>students</u> **are** going to get an A.*

4. **Either/Or**, **Neither/Nor**, **Or**. When the subjects differ in numbers, the noun closest to the verb dictates if it is singular or plural.

   *Neither I nor my <u>friends</u> **are** going anywhere for winter break.*
   *Either the dogs or the <u>cat</u> **has** ripped the couch.*

   In a compound subject joined by "or," the number of the noun after "or" determines whether the verb is singular or plural.

   *<u>Emily</u> or <u>Dan</u> **is** able to drive the car.*
   *<u>Emily</u> and <u>Dan</u> **are** able to drive the car.*

5. **Few**, **Many**, **Several**, **Both**, **All**, **Some**. When these determiners are used with a countable noun, the verb is plural.

   *Few people **are** turning in the assignment late.*

   When they are used with a non-count noun, the verb is singular.

   *Some sand **is** missing from the pile.*

6. **Each**, **Every**, **No**. If "each," "every," or "no" is before the subject, the verb will be singular.

*Every <u>table</u> and <u>chair</u> **has** to be put back in the right formation.*
*No <u>student</u> **is** allowed to skip a final exam.*
*Each <u>person</u> **is** required to sign in.*

7. **Collective Nouns.** For collective nouns, such as "population," "audience," "family," and "group," subject-verb agreement can be tricky because it depends on the writer's intent.
    *The <u>group</u> [as a unit] **was** late to the field trip*
    *The <u>group</u> [of individuals] **are** late to the field trip.*

8. **Subject and Verb Separated by a Phrase.** When the subject and verb are separated by a phrase (as well as, along with, besides, not, etc.), the verb should always agree with the subject, even if the phrase contains a noun whose number does not match the subject's.
    *<u>Mayor Pete</u>, along with staffers, **is** coming to speak at the Harris School.*
    *<u>Politicians</u> (along with an aide) **are** coming to visit the Harris School.*

Using the correct verb tense

English verb tenses are sometimes difficult to get right. The verb tense you use should remain consistent, throughout sentences, throughout paragraphs, and throughout the entire body of whatever you are writing—unless you have a good reason to change it. For example:

- **Incorrect**: When my roommate **goes** to the store, she **bought** a treat for everyone. *Goes* is in the present tense and *bought* is in the past tense, and there is no good reason to change the tense in the sentence.
- **Correct Option 1**: When my roommate **goes** to the store, she **buys** a treat for everyone. (Both verbs are in the present tense.)
- **Correct Option 2**: When my roommate **went** to the store, she **bought** a treat for everyone. (Both verbs are in the present tense.)

Here's a quick overview of the different tenses in English and how to use them correctly.

- **Present tense** indicates that an action is taking place at the time you express it or that an action occurs regularly.
  - We **study** for exams at the library.
- **Past tense** indicates that an action is completed and has already taken place.
  - My family **moved** to Chicago in 2015.
  - During the whole quarter, he **wondered** how learning analytical politics would help his career in the future.
- **Future tense** indicates that an action will or is likely to take place.
  - Later today I **will work** on my programming assignment.
- **Present perfect tense** indicates that an action is taking place at the time you express it or that an action occurs regularly.
  - I **have spoken** with my academic advisor about my course selection.
  - She **has donated** extensively to the University of Chicago [an action that began in the past and extends into the present].
- **Past perfect tense** indicates an action occurring before a certain time in the past.
  - By the winter of 2018, she **had completed** all the credits required to graduate.
- **Future perfect** indicates that an action will be finished by a certain time.
  - By Thursday, we **will have finished** this problem set.
- **Present progressive tense** indicates that something is happening at the time you express it.
  - Robert **is working** hard, and his teammate **is watching** lazily.
- **Past progressive tense** indicates two kinds of past action.
  - His lecture **was becoming** increasingly boring and difficult [a continuing action in the past].
  - One guy interrupted the professor multiple times today while she **was introducing** the class material [an action occurring at the same time in the past as another action].

- **Future progressive tense** indicates a continuing in the future.
  - The TAs **will be grading** all assignments.
- **Present perfect progressive tense** indicates action continuing from the past into the present and possibly into the future.
  - Students **have been waiting** for their grades for over two weeks.
- **Past perfect progressive tense** indicates that a past action went on until another occurred.
  - Before her promotion, she **had been working** on introducing quiet study space in school.
- **Future perfect progressive tense** indicates that an action will continue until a certain future time.
  - On Tuesday I **will have been working** on this paper for six weeks.

WORD USAGE

Here are some words commonly misused with respect to their meaning:

- **Aggravate** means "to make worse." It does not mean to "annoy."
- **Anticipate** means "to prepare for a contingency." It does not mean just "expect."
- **Anxious** means "uneasy," not "eager."
- **Blackmail** means "to extort by threatening to reveal damaging information." It does not mean simply "coerce."
- **Cohort** means "a group who attends something." It does not mean a single accompanying person.
- **Comprise** means "to include." It is not synonymous with "constitute."
- **Continuous** means "without interruption." It is not synonymous with "continual," which means an activity continued through time with interruptions.
- **Disinterested** means "neutral." It does not mean "uninterested."
- **Enormity** has the meaning of something "hugely bad." It does not refer to large size neutrally.
- **Fortuitous** means "by chance." It does not mean "fortunate."

- **Fulsome** means "sickeningly excessive." It does not mean just "much."
- **Notorious** means "known for bad behavior." It does not mean "famous."

Check to see that you use the following words in the right context.

Admission, admittance

- "Admission" implies enrollment or access to rights or privileges.
  - His admission to the society shows his standing.
- "Admittance" is limited to actual physical entrance.
  - He could not gain admittance to the grounds.

Affect, effect

- "Affect" as a verb means to influence. "Effect" as a verb means to bring about or to accomplish. "Effect" as a noun means result or consequence.
  - The bill cannot affect us, although it may effect great change as soon as the law goes into effect.

Among, between

- "Among" indicates a relationship for three or more things or an undetermined multitude ("honor among thieves").
  - The treaty divided the land among the Navajo, Hopi, and Ute tribes.
  - Poverty is common among those with little education.
- "Between" indicates a one-to-one relationship, usually involving two elements ("between you and me"). However, "between" is also appropriate for more than two objects if multiple one-to-one relationships exist ("trade between members of the European union").
  - An agreement between the Senate and the House was reached.
  - He could not distinguish between morning, noon, and night.
  - Negotiations between DEA, the FBI, and the CIA are at an impasse.

And, or, and/or

- "And" joins two or more items.
  - ○ I will have cream and sugar in my coffee.
- "Or" indicates an alternative between two items but does not necessarily exclude one from the other.
  - ○ Will you have cream or sugar in your coffee?
  - ○ The weather forecast calls for rain or sleet tomorrow.
- "And/or" is not a term used in standard English. It is a legalism meaning "x or y, or both x and y," as in:
  - ○ She will go to Paris, Athens, or both.
- Do not use "and/or" unless using a direct quotation that includes the term.

Assure, ensure, insure

- "Assure" implies the removal of doubt from a person's mind and must have a personal object.
  - ○ To assure the auditors of the facts, I gave them the records.
- "Ensure" indicates the making certain of an outcome and refers to events.
  - ○ Directors ensure that report information is accurate.
- "Insure" means to guarantee against loss by a contingent event.
  - ○ Jane insured the package she mailed.

Based on, on the basis of

- Best uses for "based on":
  - ○ as a transitive verb: "They based their position on military precedent."
  - ○ in an adjectival sense: "a sophisticated thriller based on a Mark Twain story."
- Avoid using it as an adverb: "Raters are adjusted annually based on the 91-day Treasury bill." Instead, use "Rates are adjusted annually on the basis of the 91-day Treasury bill."
- Be wary of using "based on" at the beginning of a sentence. If it doesn't modify the subject, a dangling phrase is the result.
  - ○ *Wrong*: Based on our recommendations, the board voted for the plan. (The board isn't based on the recommendation.)

- ○ *Better*: The board, following our recommendations, adopted the plan.
- If the subject is not based on something, try "because of," "from," "according to," "in light of," "given," or a different construction.
- Instead of "on the basis of," use the more concise "on," "by," "after," "because of," or "from," as appropriate.

Beside, besides

- "Beside" means by the side of.
  - ○ Beside the screen was a knob to control the contrast.
- "Besides" means in addition to.
  - ○ Besides outlining the weaknesses, the report summarizes the strengths.

Both, each

- "Both" means two considered together.
  - ○ Both cost $10.
- "Each" means any number taken one at a time.
  - ○ Each of them costs $5.

Compare to, with

- "Compare to" is used when the intent is to liken things that are dissimilar.
  - ○ Shall I compare thee to a summer's day? (Shakespeare)
- "Compare with" is used to compare or contrast.
  - ○ Compare this year's progress with last year's.

Comprise, constitute

- The whole comprises the parts.
  - ○ The committee comprises five subcommittees.
- Several parts constitute the whole.
  - ○ Five subcommittees constitute the full committee.
- *Note*: Do not use "is comprised of." Use "consists of" or "is composed of" instead.
  - ○ The committee consists of (or "is composed of") five sub-committees.

Continual, continuous

- "Continual" means periodically recurring, with pauses or breaks. "Continuous" means continuing without interruption.
  - The weather forecast was for continual cloudiness with periods of sunshine.
  - Without aspirin, his pain was continuous.

Copyright and trademark

- Instead of trademark names, use generic product descriptions.
  - For example, use "cotton swabs" instead of "Q-tips."
- Only use a trademark name when it is necessary to refer to a particular product brand. In those instances, the trademark name should be used as an adjective, followed by a general description of the product.
  - "Q-tips® cotton swabs"; "Scotchgard® fabric protector."
- Use the symbols only one time in a document unless there is enough distance between the first and subsequent uses. For reports, if a symbol appears on the highlights page and in the report text, use it in both places since the highlights page is intended to be freestanding. If a symbol appears in a footnote first, use the symbol there but also use it on first reference in the text (readers may not have read the footnote).
- Registered trademarks may be found on the websites of the US Patent and Trademark Office and the International Trademark Association.

Different from, than

- Only use "different from." Do not use "different than."
  - The program was different from what it was 10 years ago.
  - The respondents in Denver are different from those in Detroit.

Disinterested, uninterested

- "Disinterested" means to be neutral or unbiased. "Uninterested" means to be indifferent, to lack interest in.

- The agency needed disinterested officials to monitor the results.
- I am uninterested in politics.

Due to, because of

- "Due to" is one of the most misused terms in government writing. Do not use "due to" in place of "because of," "owing to," "on account of," "stemming from," and similar phrases.
  - Grammatically, "due" is an adjective that should be attached only to a noun or pronoun.
    - *Wrong*: The program failed due to insufficient funding. ("Due" does not modify the noun "program.")
    - *Permissible*: The program's failure was due to insufficient funding. ("Due" modifies "failure.")
    - *Better (more active and concise)*: The program failed because of insufficient funding.

E.g., i.e.

- The Latin abbreviation "i.e." means "that is" and "i.e." means "for example."
- In regular text, use the English words, but the Latin abbreviations may be used when they appear inside parentheses or in notes.

Either . . . or, neither . . . nor

- "Either . . . or" and "neither . . . nor" are correlative conjunctions, which means they join two terms that should be parallel in form. In these constructions, the verb should agree with the nearest subject. When plural and singular terms are involved, it is usually smoother to place the plural term second.
  - Either the coach or the players have to go.
- Avoid joining three or more terms with "either/or" and "neither/nor." Here, for example, simply use "or."
  - The official planned to visit BLM, DOE, or EPA.

Farther, further, furthermore

- "Farther" expresses physical distance.
  - ○ I can walk no farther.
- "Further" means to a greater degree or extent.
  - ○ Expect no further assistance from me.
- "Furthermore" means in addition or besides and is generally used at the beginning of a sentence.
  - ○ The legislation did not make the mandate clear. Furthermore, the agency did not have enough resources to complete the task.

Fewer, less

- Use "fewer" for people and items you can individually count.
  - ○ Fewer than 100 respondents reported the problem.
  - ○ Fewer accidents were reported.
  - ○ *Note*: If there is only one item, use, for example, "one response fewer."
- "Less" is used for things not considered discrete items.
  - ○ periods of time (e.g., less than 10 years ago).
  - ○ amounts of money (e.g., less than $10 million).
  - ○ quantities that must be measured (e.g., less than a teaspoon).
  - ○ percentages (e.g., less than 5 percent of the respondents).
  - ○ extent (e.g., less effort was required).

Hopefully

- "Hopefully" means in a hopeful manner or "with hope" but is frequently misused in the sense of "we hope" or "it is hoped."
  - ○ *Wrong*: Provisions were enacted to increase the limits on defined contribution plans, a step that hopefully might spur employers to save more.
  - ○ *Right*: Provisions were enacted to increase the limits on defined contribution plans, a step that officials hoped might spur employers to save more.

Imply, infer

- Speakers, writers, or facts imply: they attribute one thing to another.
  - Smoke implies fire.
  - He said the high response rate implied success.
- Readers or listeners infer something: they conclude or surmise.
  - The staff inferred from the memo that the director wanted them to take action.

Percent, percentage

- In text, use a numeral with "percent." Use the percentage sign (%) only in tables and figures.
- Do not mix fractions and percentages in the same context.
- Distinguish between "percent" as denoting a specific quantity and "percentage" as denoting an unspecified quantity:
  - The program was cut by a large percentage.
- "A 5 percent difference" and "a 5 percentage point difference" do not mean the same thing.
  - A difference that amounts to 5 percent of the total is a "5 percent difference."
  - The difference between 4 percent and 8 percent is "a 4 percentage point difference." (Note that "percent" is repeated with each numeral.)

Practical, practicable

- "Practical" applies to persons and things and relates to actual practice or action, rather than theory: knowledgeable as a result of practice, useful, and sensible.
- "Practicable" applies to something that has not yet been worked out or fully tested but that seems feasible and usable or can be put into practice.
  - An official can be practical but not practicable.
  - The election will be announced as soon as practicable.
  - A suggestion can be both practical and practicable.

Principal, principle

- "Principal" is a noun and an adjective that denotes the chief person or thing that has controlling authority or is of primary importance.
- "Principle" is a noun that denotes a comprehensive and fundamental law, doctrine, or assumption.
  - The principal member of the board reminded us of the principles of committee conduct.

Quality

- Avoid using "quality" as an adjective. It is best used strictly as a noun.
  - *Avoid*: "XYZ is a quality program."
  - *Better*: "The program is of high quality."

Scientific names

- Capitalize genus but lowercase species.
- Both genus and species are italicized: *Ficus bengalensis, Pan troglodytes, Homo sapiens*.
- However, when the Latin names have been turned into English nouns or adjectives, the names should not be capitalized or italicized:
  - Epidemic strains of pneumococcus are common, but penicillin is effective against most pneumonia organisms.

That, which

- "That" introduces restrictive clauses that cannot be removed from a sentence without destroying its meaning.
  - Ships that are unseaworthy should be scrapped.
- "Which" introduces nonrestrictive clauses, which are set off by commas, to show that the clauses can be lifted from a sentence without destroying its meaning.
  - The agency's policy, which expired in June 2011, may be renewed.

- *Common mistakes with* which *and* that:
    - The year which our daughter was born was a great year. (wrong; restrictive)
    - The year that our daughter was born was a great year. (correct)
    - This book, that was written last November, is a great read. (wrong; unrestrictive)
    - This book, which was written last November, is a great read. (correct)
    - Any book which gets him reading is worth having. (wrong; restrictive)
    - Any book that gets him reading is worth having. (correct)

Then, than

- Use "then" when you're talking about something that has to do with sequence or consequence. For example:
    - I couldn't answer the phone because I was in class then. (at that time)
    - We got gas and then set off on the road trip. (next in time)
    - First you need to get your master's degree, and then you can find a job. (in addition; moreover)
    - If the weather is bad, then my flight will get canceled. (in that case; accordingly)
- Use "than" when you're making a comparison between people, things, etc. For example:
    - Spring quarter is better than winter quarter.
    - She works faster than I do in the Coding Lab.
- *Common mistakes with* then *and* than:
    - He has less chocolate then I have. (wrong; comparative)
    - He has less chocolate than I have. (correct)
    - I would rather eat then sleep. (wrong; comparative)
    - I would rather eat than sleep. (correct)
    - I would prefer to eat sooner rather then later. (wrong; comparative)
    - I would prefer to eat sooner rather than later. (correct)

This

- For clarity, give "this" a noun for a partner.
  - *Draft*: This complies with GAO regulations.
  - *Revision*: This project complies with GAO regulations.

Toward, towards

- "Toward" is favored in the United States
- "Towards" is favored in Canada and the United Kingdom.

Under way, underway

- The adverb "under way" is two words.
  - The project is under way
- "Underway," an adjective, is rare and usually awkward: "an underway refueling."

Via

- "Via" means "by way of," not "by means of."
  - *Right*: Flying to Paris via London.
  - *Wrong*: Sent via email.

Vis-à-vis

- "Vis-à-vis" is usually best avoided. The term means "face to face" or "in relation to," but it is often misused to mean "concerning."
  - *Right*: Figures should be checked for appropriateness vis-à-vis the text.
  - *Wrong*: The case demonstrates the court's attitude vis-à-vis age discrimination in employee benefit plans.

Who, whom, that

- Use "who" in reference to persons and "that" in reference to things.
  - Who returned the questionnaire?
  - We contacted the two agencies that did not respond to the survey.

- When a person is the subject of a sentence or clause, use "who."
  - The official who provided the document did not work for the program.
- When a person is the object of a sentence or clause, use "whom."
  - Whom did you interview?

Acknowledgments

An author friend of mine once told me that books are never finished. They are, in all honesty, surrendered by authors who had to send a manuscript to their editor. They are, in other words, products of exhaustion. Now that I've written a few books, I can attest to this. It was true for the first edition of this book, and it's true for this edition, too. I wrote myself out the first time around, and I will write myself out when (fingers crossed!) I someday start on the third edition of this book.

I am, as ever, grateful to my editor, Robin Coleman, who, after three books together, has become a trusted friend and advisor. This book would not have been possible without the support of the University of Chicago's Harris School of Public Policy and all of the brilliant, passionate students I've worked with there. Thank you to Katherine Baicker, Kate Shannon Biddle, Terri Brady, Ethan Bueno de Mesquita, Misho Ceko, Andrew Dawson, Krisinda Doherty, Jeremy Edwards, Anthony Fowler, Karen Gahl-Mills, Mohamad Hafez, Peggy Harper, Michelle Hoereth, Jamia Jowers, Ryan Kellogg, Brandon Kurzweg, Shilin Liu, Jen Lombardo, Luis Martinez, Adam McGriffin, Billy Morgan, Dave Stone, Paula Worthington, and Austin Wright. It also would not have been possible without the help, faith, and guidance of several friends and colleagues who showed me how to find the voice and the distance from which the stories in this book needed to be told. Thank you Chad Broughton, Sorcha Brophy, Isabeau Dasho, Will Gossin, and Nigel O'Hearn.

I'd also like to thank my wife, Ashley, for all her love and support, without which I haven't a clue where I'd be today.

Notes

Foreword

1. Katherine Baicker et al., "The Oregon Experiment—Effects of Medicaid on Clinical Outcomes," *New England Journal of Medicine* 368 (May 2, 2013): 1713–22, http://doi.org/10.1056/NEJMsa1212321.
2. Annie Lowrey, "Medicaid Access Increases Use of Care, Study Finds," *New York Times*, May 1, 2013, https://www.nytimes.com/2013/05/02/business /study-finds-health-care-use-rises-with-expanded-medicaid.html.
3. Ezra Klein, "Here's What the Oregon Medicaid Study Really Said," *Washington Post*, May 2, 2013, https://www.washingtonpost.com/news/wonk/wp /2013/05/02/heres-what-the-oregon-medicaid-study-really-said/.
4. Chuck Sheketoff, "Oregon's Lesson to the Nation: Medicaid Works," Oregon Center for Public Policy, May 4, 2013, https://www.ocpp.org/2013/05/04 /blog20130504-oregon-lesson-nation-medicaid-works/.
5. Michael F. Cannon, "Oregon Study Throws a Stop Sign in Front of ObamaCare's Medicaid Expansion," *Cato at Liberty* (blog), May 1, 2013, https://www.cato.org/blog/oregon-study-throws-stop-sign-front -obamacares-medicaid-expansion.
6. *Testimony of Michael Tanner, Senior Fellow, Cato Institute before the Kansas Senate Committee on Public Health and Welfare* (March 21, 2017), http:// kslegislature.org/li_2018/b2017_18/committees/ctte_s_phw_1/documents /testimony/20170321_08.pdf.
7. Avik Roy, "Oregon Study: Medicaid 'Had No Significant Effect' on Health Outcomes vs. Being Uninsured," *Forbes*, May 2, 2013, https://www.forbes .com/sites/theapothecary/2013/05/02/oregon-study-medicaid-had-no -significant-effect-on-health-outcomes-vs-being-uninsured/#18b309d46043.
8. Dashiell Bennett, "How to Use the Oregon Medicaid Study to Your Ideological Advantage," *Atlantic,* May 2, 2013, https://www.theatlantic.com/poli tics/archive/2013/05/oregon-medicaid-study/315672/.
9. Katherine Baicker and Amy Finkelstein, "What's the Story with Obamacare," *Health Affairs,* December 9, 2016, https://www.healthaffairs. org/do/10.1377/hblog20161209.057856/full/.

Introduction

1. "Document: Read the Whistle-Blower Complaint," *New York Times,* September 26, 2019, https://www.nytimes.com/interactive/2019/09/26/us/politics /whistle-blower-complaint.html?module=inline.
2. "Document: Read the Whistle-Blower Complaint."
3. Special Counsel Robert S. Mueller III, *Report on the Investigation into Russian Interference in the 2016 Presidential Election* (Washington, DC: United States Government Publishing Office, March 2019), https://www

.govinfo.gov/content/pkg/GPO-SCREPORT-MUELLER/pdf/GPO
-SCREPORT-MUELLER.pdf.

4. Kyle Cheney, "Nadler: 'There Certainly Is' Justification for Impeaching
Trump," *Politico,* May 31, 2019, https://www.politico.com/story/2019/05/31
/donald-trump-impeachment-jerry-nadler-1348679.

5. "Mueller Finds No Collusion with Russia, Leaves Obstruction Question
Open," American Bar Association, n.d., https://www.americanbar.org/news
/abanews/aba-news-archives/2019/03/mueller-concludes-investigation/;
for the attorney general's letter to Congress, see https://www.scribd.com
/document/402973349/AG-March-24-2019-Letter-to-House-and-Senate
-Judiciary-Committees#from_embed.

6. Jeffrey Toobin, "Why the Mueller Investigation Failed," *New Yorker,* June 29,
2020, https://www.newyorker.com/magazine/2020/07/06/why-the-mueller
-investigation-failed.

7. Quoted in Toobin, "Why the Mueller Investigation Failed."

8. Mark Mazzetti and Nicholas Fandos, "G.O.P.-Led Senate Panel Details Ties
between 2016 Trump Campaign and Russia," *New York Times,* August 18,
2020, https://www.nytimes.com/2020/08/18/us/politics/senate-intelligence
-russian-interference-report.html.

9. Greg Miller, Karoun Demirjian, and Ellen Nakashima, "Senate Report
Details Security Risk Posed by 2016 Trump Campaign's Russia Contacts,"
Washington Post, August 18, 2020, https://www.washingtonpost.com
/national-security/senate-intelligence-trump-russia-report/2020/08/18
/62a7573e-e093-11ea-b69b-64f7b0477ed4_story.html.

10. "Document: Read the Whistle-Blower Complaint."

11. "Document: Read the Whistle-Blower Complaint."

12. George Orwell, "Politics and the English Language," in *Why I Write* (New
York: Penguin Books, 1984), 102–3.

13. John O'Hayre, *Gobbledygook Has Gotta Go* (Washington, DC: US Government Printing Office, 1966), 5, https://www.governmentattic.org/15docs
/Gobbledygook_Has_Gotta_Go_1966.pdf.

14. For a history of plain language in the US government, see "History and
Timeline," plainlanguage.gov, n.d., https://www.plainlanguage.gov/about
/history/.

15. "Guidelines for President Clinton's Memo," plainlanguage.gov, n.d., https://
www.plainlanguage.gov/about/history/memo-guidelines/.

16. Plain Writing Act of 2010, Pub. L. No. 111-274, 124 Stat. 2861 (2010), https://
www.govinfo.gov/content/pkg/PLAW-111publ274/pdf/PLAW-111publ274.pdf.

Chapter 1. Clear Thinking Leads to Clear Writing

1. Peter Suderman, "It's Time to Bust Police Unions," *Reason,* June 3, 2020,
https://reason.com/2020/06/03/its-time-to-bust-police-unions/.

2. "How Police Union Contracts Block Accountability," Police Union Contract
Project, n.d., https://www.checkthepolice.org/#project.

3. Mariame Kaba, "Yes, We Mean Literally Abolish the Police," *New York Times,* June 12, 2020, https://www.nytimes.com/2020/06/12/opinion/sunday /floyd-abolish-defund-police.html.

4. Leana S. Wen, "Instead of 'Defund' the Police, Imagine a Broader Role for Them with Public Health," *Washington Post,* June 12, 2020, https://www .washingtonpost.com/opinions/2020/06/12/instead-defund-police-imagine -broader-role-them-public-health/.

5. Ranjani Chakraborty, "What 'Defund the Police' Really Means," Vox, June 26, 2020, https://www.vox.com/2020/6/26/21303849/what-defund-the-police -really-means.

6. Chakraborty, "What 'Defund the Police' Really Means."

7. Jeff Asher and Ben Horwitz, "How Do the Police Actually Spend Their Time?," *New York Times,* June 19, 2020, https://www.nytimes.com/2020/06/19 /upshot/unrest-police-time-violent-crime.html.

8. Chakraborty, "What 'Defund the Police' Really Means."

9. Chakraborty, "What 'Defund the Police' Really Means."

10. Monica Davey, "Chicago to Hire Many More Police, but Effect on Crime Is Debated," *New York Times,* September 21, 2016, https://www.nytimes.com /2016/09/22/us/chicago-to-hire-many-more-police-but-effect-on-crime -is-debated.html.

11. Davey, "Chicago to Hire Many More Police."

12. Independent Monitoring Team, *Independent Monitoring Report 2,* June 18, 2020, https://cpdmonitoringteam.com/wp-content/uploads/2020/06/2020 _06_18-Independent-Monitoring-Report-2-filed.pdf.

13. Cure Violence, "Where We Work," n.d., https://cvg.org/where-we-work/.

14. David B. Henry, Shannon Knoblauch, and Rannveig Sigurvinsdottier, "The Effect of Intensive CeaseFire Intervention on Crime in Four Chicago Police Beats: Quantitative Assessment," September 11, 2014, https:// 1vp6u534z5kr2qmr0w11t7ub-wpengine.netdna-ssl.com/wp-content /uploads/2019/09/McCormick_CreaseFire_Quantitative_Report_091114 .pdf.

15. Leana S. Wen and M. Cooper Lloyd, "Baltimore Is Attacking the Roots of Violence with Public Health Measures—and Saving Lives," *Scientific American,* November 1, 2016, https://www.scientificamerican.com/article /baltimore-is-attacking-the-roots-of-violence-with-public-health -measures-mdash-and-saving-lives/.

16. Alayna Alvarez, "Treating People as Patients: Denver Police's Partnership with Mental Health Professionals Is Working, It Says," *Colorado Politics,* October 24, 2019, https://www.coloradopolitics.com/denver/treating -people-as-patients-denver-police-s-partnership-with-mental/article _ef59384c-f669-11e9-b84b-7f9529932a3f.html.

17. Alayna Alvarez, "Denver's Police Partnership with Mental Health Professionals Likely to Extend through 2020," *Colorado Politics,* December 19, 2019, updated January 2, 2020, https://www.coloradopolitics.com/denver

/denver-s-police-partnership-with-mental-health-professionals-likely-to
-extend-through-2020/article_850ac5fe-21e9-11ea-8c40-7f89bdf9461c.html.

18. Alvarez, "Denver's Police Partnership with Mental Health Professionals."

19. Michael J. D. Vermeer, Dulani Woods, and Brian A. Jackson, "Would Law
Enforcement Leaders Support Defunding the Police? Probably—*If* Communities Ask Police to Solve Fewer Problems," Rand Corporation, August 2020,
https://www.rand.org/pubs/perspectives/PEA108-1.html.

20. Peter Jamison, "This California City Defunded Its Police Force. Killings
by Officers Soared," *Washington Post,* June 23, 2020, https://www
.washingtonpost.com/local/public-safety/this-california-city-defunded
-its-police-force-killings-by-officers-soared/2020/06/22/253eeddc-b198
-11ea-856d-5054296735e5_story.html.

21. Jay Heinrichs, *Thank You for Arguing: What Aristotle, Lincoln, and Homer
Simpson Can Teach Us about the Art of Persuasion* (New York: Three River
Press, 2013), 30.

22. Heinrichs, *Thank You for Arguing,* 37.

23. Workers Center for Racial Justice, "Proposal for Equitable Public Safety
Reinvestment," n.d., https://599e3d43-54d2-4ecd-8b5d-ec54ea312ee9
.filesusr.com/ugd/dd589b_941489993e74415faad4a35e5a4bc427.pdf.

Chapter 2. Mastering Deductive, Evaluative, and Prescriptive Policy Answers

1. Katherine W. Phillips, "How Diversity Works," *Scientific American,* October
2014.

2. W. Gary Simpson, David A. Carter, and Frank D'Souza, "What Do We Know
about Women on Boards?," *Journal of Applied Finance* 20, no. 2 (2010),
https://ssrn.com/abstract=2693058; Deborah L. Rhode and Amanda K.
Packel, "Diversity on Corporate Boards: How Much Difference Does Difference Make," *Delaware Journal of Corporate Law* 39, no. 2 (2014): 377–426.

3. University of Chicago Crime and Education Labs, *Choose to Change: Your
Mind, Your Game,* research brief, February 2020, https://urbanlabs.uchicago
.edu/attachments/dd47d0bf9f85c9543e871d03b25fa1dcc8ee779f/store
/cf2bff02b6f54df79d84cd3c2b20d7bd0ec398cdd7a4de0744e6e8860d6f
/Choose+to+Change+Research+Brief.pdf.

4. University of Chicago Crime and Education Labs, *University of Chicago
Crime and Education Labs' Evaluation of Choose to Change Suggests Promise
in Improving Life Outcomes for Chicago's Youth,* press release, n.d., https://
urbanlabs.uchicago.edu/attachments/7077a511c389b24215c9ebf12c4e88
be432e4581/store/edc520956b81e07f09067f0f504657e0915454dbdd1340
ded13b7f388241/C2C+Press+Release.pdf.

5. University of Chicago Crime and Education Labs, *University of Chicago
Crime and Education Labs' Evaluation of Choose to Change.*

6. University of Chicago Crime and Education Labs, *University of Chicago
Crime and Education Labs' Evaluation of Choose to Change.*

7. US Government Accountability Office, "Pension Benefit Guarantee

Corporation: Redesigned Premium Structure Could Better Align Rates with Risk from Plan Sponsors," GAO-13-58, November 7, 2012, https://www.gao .gov/products/GAO-13-58.

8. Pension Benefit Guarantee Corporation, "PBGC Releases FY 2019 Annual Report," November 18, 2019, https://www.pbgc.gov/news/press/releases /pr19-12.

Chapter 3. Meeting the Unique Needs of Your Reader

1. Farhad Manjoo, *True Enough: Learning to Live in a Post-Fact Society* (Hoboken, NJ: John Wiley & Sons, 2008), 52–53.

2. Maria Milosh et al. "Unmasking Partisanship: How Polarization Influences Public Responses to Collective Risk" (working paper, Becker Friedman Institute for Economics at the University of Chicago, July 31, 2020), https:// bfi.uchicago.edu/working-paper/unmasking-partisanship-how-polarization -influences-public-responses-to-collective-risk/.

3. National Center for Education Statistics, "Program for the International Assessment of Adult Competencies Results," 2017, https://nces.ed.gov /surveys/piaac/current_results.asp#international.

4. Philip Bump, "Trump Actually Doesn't Appear to Understand How Bad the Pandemic Is," *Washington Post*, August 4, 2020, https://www.washington post.com/politics/2020/08/04/trump-actually-doesnt-appear-understand -how-bad-pandemic-is/.

5. "Axios on HBO: President Trump Exclusive Interview," YouTube, uploaded August 3, 2020, https://www.youtube.com/watch?v=zaaTZkqsaxY&feature =youtu.be.

6. Daniel Kahneman, *Thinking, Fast and Slow* (New York: Farrar, Straus and Giroux, 2011), 20–21.

Chapter 4. Developing Stronger Policy Recommendations Using Human-Centered Design

1. "A Short History of U.S. International Food Assistance," US Department of State, n.d., https://2009-2017.state.gov/p/eur/ci/it/milanexpo2015/c67068 .htm.

2. US Agency for International Development, *Emergency Food Security Program—Fiscal Year 2017 Report to Congress*, n.d., https://www.usaid.gov /sites/default/files/documents/1867/PA00SW3C.pdf.

3. Congressional Research Service, *U.S. International Food Assistance: An Overview*, R45422, December 6, 2018, https://fas.org/sgp/crs/row/R45422.pdf.

4. Eric C. Lentz, Simone Passarelli, and Christopher B. Barrett, "The Timeliness and Cost-Effectiveness of the Local and Regional Procurement of Food Aid," *World Development* 49 (2013): 9–18, http://dx.doi.org/10.1016 /j.worlddev.2013.01.017.

5. Maya Gainer, "2018-19 IDEV Roundtable: The Evolution of Food Assistance," *Perspectives*, a publication of the International Development Program at

Johns Hopkins School of Advanced International Studies, May 8, 2019, http://www.saisperspectives.com/idev-roundtable-series/2019/5/8/2018-19-idev-roundtable-the-evolution-of-food-assistance.

6. Government Accountability Office, *International Cash-Based Food Assistance: USAID Has Established Processes to Monitor Cash and Voucher Projects, but Data Limitations Impede Evaluation*, GAO-16-819, September 20, 2016, https://www.gao.gov/products/GAO-16-819.

7. Government Accountability Office, *International Cash-Based Food Assistance*.

8. International Food Policy Research Institute, *How the United States Benefits from Agricultural and Food Security Investments in Developing Countries*, 2019, https://www.aplu.org/library/how-the-united-states-benefits-from-agricultural-and-food-security-investments-in-developing-countries/file.

9. Bob Stallman, "Op-Ed: Let's Keep the Food in Food Aid," *Agri-Pulse Communications*, May 14, 2013, https://www.agri-pulse.com/articles/2847-op-ed-let-s-keep-the-food-in-food-aid.

10. Claire Provost, "US Food Aid: The Special Interests Blocking Reform," *Guardian,* July 19, 2012, https://www.theguardian.com/global-development/2012/jul/19/us-food-aid-special-interests-reform.

11. Nathan Nunn and Nancy Qian, "US Food Aid and Civil Conflict," *American Economic Review* 104, no. 6 (2014): 1630–66, http://dx.doi.org/10.1257/aer.104.6.1630.

12. Nunn and Qian, "US Food Aid and Civil Conflict," 1630.

13. Jerry Hagstrom, "Corker Urges Food Aid Changes," DTN.com, October 23, 2017, https://www.dtnpf.com/agriculture/web/ag/news/article/2017/10/23/wheat-growers-defend-current-program.

14. Shmuel Lederman, *Hannah Arendt and Participatory Democracy: A People's Utopia* (London: Palgrave Macmillan, 2019), 77.

15. Government Accountability Office, *Government Auditing Standards: 2018 Revision*, GAO-18-568G, July 2018, 115, https://www.gao.gov/assets/700/693136.pdf.

16. Provost, "US Food Aid."

17. Aaron Wildavsky, *Speaking Truth to Power: The Art and Craft of Policy Analysis* (New York: Transaction, 1987), 5.

18. Wildavsky, *Speaking Truth to Power*, 16.

Chapter 5. How to Haunt Your Readers

1. David Chrisinger, "White Supremacy in the Military 'Like a Drop of Cyanide in Your Drink,'" The War Horse, March 18, 2020, https://thewarhorse.org/the-invisible-reach-of-white-supremacy/.

2. Lynh Bui, "'I Am Dreaming of a Way to Kill Almost Every Last Person on Earth': A Self-Proclaimed White Nationalist Planned a Mass Terrorist Attack, the Government Says," *Washington Post*, February 20, 2019, https://www.washingtonpost.com/local/public-safety/self-proclaimed-white-nationalist

-planned-mass-terror-attack-government-says-i-am-dreaming-of-a-way-to
-kill-almost-every-last-person-on-earth/2019/02/20/61daf6b8-3544-11e9
-af5b-b51b7ff322e9_story.html.

3. Paul Duggan, "Coast Guard Lt. Christopher Hasson Sentenced to 13 Years
   in Alleged Terror Plot," *Washington Post*, January 31, 2020, https://www
   .washingtonpost.com/local/public-safety/coast-guard-lt-christopher-has
   son-set-to-be-sentenced-in-alleged-terror-plot/2020/01/31/d01b048a
   -43ce-11ea-aa6a-083d01b3ed18_story.html.

4. Bui, " 'I Am Dreaming of a Way to Kill Almost Every Last Person on Earth.' "

5. Jane Alison, "Beyond the Narrative Arc," *Paris Review*, March 27, 2019,
   https://www.theparisreview.org/blog/2019/03/27/beyond-the-narrative
   -arc/.

6. Aristotle, *Poetics*, trans. Ingram Bywater, chap. 18.

7. Leo Shane, "Signs of White Supremacy, Extremism Up Again in Poll of
   Active-Duty Troops," *Military Times*, February 6, 2020, https://www
   .militarytimes.com/news/pentagon-congress/2020/02/06/signs-of-white
   -supremacy-extremism-up-again-in-poll-of-active-duty-troops/.

8. "Secretary Esper Holds an In-Flight Media Availability," US Department
   of Defense, December 16, 2019, https://www.defense.gov/Newsroom
   /Transcripts/Transcript/Article/2041530/secretary-esper-holds-an-in
   -flight-media-availability/.

9. Nancy Montgomery, "Neo-Nazis Excluded from Military Service by Policy,
   but Concerns Persist," *Stars and Stripes*, August 18, 2017, https://www
   .stripes.com/news/neo-nazis-excluded-from-military-service-by-policy
   -but-concerns-persist-1.483558.

10. Dave Philipps, "White Supremacism in the US Military, Explained," *New
    York Times*, February 27, 2019, https://www.nytimes.com/2019/02/27/us
    /military-white-nationalists-extremists.html.

11. "It Was My Choice to Leave Homeland Security, Selim Says," NPR, August 7,
    2017, https://www.npr.org/2017/08/07/541983688/it-was-my-choice-to
    -leave-homeland-security-selim-says; see also Tess Owen, "Trump Shut
    Down Program That Could Help Stop the Next White Nationalist Attack,"
    Vice, March 20, 2019, https://www.vice.com/en_us/article/yw8jak/trump
    -says-white-nationalism-isnt-a-threat-and-shut-down-programs-to
    -combat-it.

12. Melanie Zanona, "Trump Cuts Funds to Fight Anti–Right Wing Violence,"
    The Hill, August 14, 2017, https://thehill.com/policy/national-security
    /346552-trump-cut-funds-to-fight-anti-right-wing-violence.

13. Vera Bergengruen and W. J. Hennigan, " 'We Are Being Eaten from Within.'
    Why America Is Losing the Battle against White Nationalist Terrorism,"
    Time, August 8, 2019, https://time.com/5647304/white-nationalist
    -terrorism-united-states/.

14. *Written Testimony of Heidi L. Beirich before the [House] Armed Services
    Committee Military Personnel Subcommittee*, February 11, 2020, https://

docs.house.gov/meetings/AS/AS02/20200211/110495/HHRG-116-AS02
-Wstate-BeirichH-20200211.pdf.

15. Quoted in Derren Brown, *Happy: Why More or Less Everything Is Absolutely Fine* (London: Bantam Press, 2016), 366.

16. Tess Owen, "How an Allegedly Violent White Nationalist Spent Decades in the US Military Undetected," Vice, February 23, 2019, https://www.vice.com /en_us/article/vbwyjd/how-an-allegedly-violent-white-nationalist-spent -decades-in-the-us-military-undetected.

17. David Holthouse, "Several High Profile Racist Extremists Serve in the US Military," Southern Poverty Law Center's *Intelligence Report*, August 11, 2006, https://www.splcenter.org/fighting-hate/intelligence-report/2006 /several-high-profile-racist-extremists-serve-us-military.

Chapter 8. Coherent Paragraphs

1. William Zinsser, *On Writing Well: The Classic Guide to Writing Nonfiction*, 25th anniversary ed. (New York: HarperCollins, 2001), 73.

Chapter 9. Clear and Concise Sentences

1. Scott Sleek, "The Curse of Knowledge: Pinker Describes a Key Cause of Bad Writing," Association for Psychological Science, July 30, 2015, https:// www.psychologicalscience.org/observer/the-curse-of-knowledge-pinker -describes-a-key-cause-of-bad-writing.

2. Joseph M. Williams and Gregory G. Colomb, *Style: Lessons in Clarity and Grace*, 10th ed. (New York: Pearson, 2010), 28.

3. Hanna Thomas and Anna Hirsch, *A Progressive's Style Guide*, SumOfUs, 2016, https://interactioninstitute.org/wp-content/uploads/2016/06/Sum -Of-Us-Progressive-Style-Guide.pdf.

4. Richard Lauchman, *Plain Style: Techniques for Simple, Concise, Emphatic Business Writing* (New York: AMACOM, 1993), 65.

5. Benjamin Dreyer, *Dreyer's English: An Utterly Correct Guide to Clarity and Style* (New York: Random House, 2019), 14.

6. William Zinsser, *On Writing Well: The Classic Guide to Writing Nonfiction*, 25th anniversary ed. (New York: HarperCollins, 2001), 67.

7. Williams and Colomb, *Style*, 59.

Chapter 10. Eleven Strategies for Ruthlessly Pruning Needless Words

1. Scott Porch, "'Literally,' Emojis, and Other Trends That Aren't Destroying English," *Atlantic*, December 30, 2014, www.theatlantic.com/entertainment /archive/2014/12/steven-pinker-interview/384092/.

2. Daniel M. Oppenheimer, "Consequences of Erudite Vernacular Utilized Irrespective of Necessity: Problems with Using Long Words Needlessly," *Applied Cognitive Psychology* 20 (2006): 139–56.

3. Stephen King, *On Writing: A Memoir of the Craft*, 10th anniversary ed. (New York: Pocket Books, 2000), 118.

4. William Zinsser, *On Writing Well: The Classic Guide to Writing Nonfiction,* 25th anniversary ed. (New York: HarperCollins, 2001), 22.

5. George Orwell, "Politics and the English Language," in *Why I Write* (New York: Penguin Books, 1984), 114–15.

6. Jason Leopold, "2014 VICE News Awards: Best Use of Deflective Phrasing— Guantanamo," Vice, December 22, 2014, https://news.vice.com/article/2014 -vice-news-awards-best-use-of-deflective-phrasing-guantanamo.

7. Orwell, "Politics and the English Language," 118.

Chapter 11. Being Your Own Best Editor

1. Quoted in "The Magic of Real Revision (and How to Teach It)," *The Graide Network,* January 22, 2019, https://www.thegraidenetwork.com/blog-all /revision-strategies.

Chapter 12. Quoting and Paraphrasing Sources Properly

1. Christopher B. Barrett and Daniel G. Maxwell, *Food Aid after Fifty Years: Recasting Its Role* (New York: Routledge, 2005), 195–96.

2. Barrett and Maxwell, *Food Aid after Fifty Years,* 195.

Suggested Further Reading

My journey as a writer, editor, and teacher has been greatly influenced by some fantastic books. Here is a list of books I continue to reference in my day-to-day work.

Eugene Bardach. *A Practical Guide for Policy Analysis: The Eightfold Path to More Effective Problem Solving.* 6th ed. CQ Press, 2020.

Simon Blackburn. *On Truth.* Oxford University Press, 2018.

Kevin Dutton. *Split-Second Persuasion: The Ancient Art and New Science of Changing Minds* Houghton Mifflin Harcourt, 2011.

Benjamin Dreyer. *Dreyer's English: An Utterly Correct Guide to Clarity and Style.* Random House, 2019.

Stanley Fish. *How to Write a Sentence: And How to Read One.* HarperCollins, 1994.

Stephen King. *On Writing: A Memoir of the Craft.* 10th anniversary ed. Scribner, 2010.

Richard A. Lanham. *Revising Prose.* 5th ed. Pearson, 2006.

Richard Lauchman. *Plain Style: Techniques for Simple, Concise, Emphatic Business Writing.* AMACOM, 2008.

Farhad Manjoo. *True Enough: Learning to Live in a Post-Fact Society.* John Wiley & Sons, 2008.

Donald Murray. *Writing to Deadline: The Journalist at Work.* Heinemann, 2000.

John O'Hayre. *Gobbledygook Has Gotta Go.* Nabu, 2011.

George Orwell. *Why I Write.* Penguin, 2005.

John Ostrom and William Cook. *Paragraph Writing Simplified.* Watson-Guptill, 1994.

Steven Pinker. *The Sense of Style: The Thinking Person's Guide to Writing in the 21st Century.* Penguin, 2015.

Kevin B. Smith and Christopher W. Larimer. *The Public Policy Theory Primer.* 3rd ed. Routledge, 2018.

Deborah Stone. *Policy Paradox: The Art of Political Decision Making.* 3rd ed. W. W. Norton, 2012.

William Strunk Jr. and E. B. White. *The Elements of Style.* 4th ed. Pearson, 2000.

Thomas Whissen. *A Way with Words: A Guide for Writers.* Oxford University Press, 1982.

Aaron Wildavsky. *Speaking Truth to Power: The Art and Craft of Policy Analysis.* Transaction, 1993.

Joseph M. Williams and Gregory G. Colomb. *Style: Lessons in Clarity and Grace.* 10th ed. Pearson, 2010.

William Zinsser. *On Writing Well: The Classic Guide to Writing Nonfiction.* 25th anniversary ed. HarperCollins, 2001.

About the Author

David Chrisinger is the director of the Harris Writing Program at the University of Chicago, where he teaches policy design and communication. He also serves as the director of writing seminars and teaches memoir writing for The War Horse, an award-winning nonprofit newsroom educating the public about military service, war, and its impact. He wrote a book based on his teaching, also published by Johns Hopkins University Press, titled *Stories Are What Save Us: A Survivor's Guide to Writing about Trauma*. David was also a contributing writer for the *New York Times Magazine*'s At War column, and he writes regularly for The War Horse. His essays and articles have also appeared in several other outlets, including *Collateral*; *War, Literature & the Arts*; *UChicago Magazine*; and *Reader's Digest*, as well as in several edited anthologies.

Before coming to the University of Chicago in 2019, David spent nearly a decade working as a communications specialist for the US Government Accountability Office, where he helped write and edit public policy reports and testimonies for Congress, turning complex data into relatable narratives. The topics that his research and writing covered included primary, secondary, and higher education; retirement security; social policy; and issues related to military veterans' transitions back to civilian life. For six years David also taught public policy writing to graduate students in the Master of Public Policy Program in the Bloomberg School of Public Health at Johns Hopkins University.

From 2014 to 2017, David taught a first-of-its-kind writing seminar for student veterans at the University of Wisconsin–Stevens Point, and in 2017, he wrote an instructor's manual for his class that is now available for adoption at every campus in the University of Wisconsin System. In 2016, David edited a collection of his students' essays, *See Me for Who I Am*, that is helping to bridge the cultural gap dividing his veteran students from those who have not served.

David is also writing a book for Penguin Press on Ernie Pyle, the famed World War II correspondent who followed front-line soldiers from North Africa to Italy, in France, and in the Pacific.

Index